Blessing to you Always

I Am a Father

Forever

D1736231

Hope this book ~, you be the best Dad you can be

Glen Warren

A. J. Warren

Dedication

This book is dedicated to my (late) parents, Archie and Magdalene Warren. They taught me to love, forgive, treat people fairly and believe in myself. Along with that, I learned from them that with education, determination, and hard work, nothing is impossible. They also taught me how to be in right standing with God, not only with my words but also in my deeds.

To my wife, Angela Hawkins-Warren, to my three children Glen II, (bonus daughter) Courtney Anthony, and Celeste, and to my (bonus son) Montel. To my six grandchildren, Christopher, Jayden, Dylan, McKenzie, Brycen, and (bonus granddaughter) London. Also to my six siblings, Earlene, (Thurman) Aaron, Priscilla, Tommy, (late) Kenneth, and Carol. I am so blessed to be born into this loving and supporting family.

And finally, to all of Fathers Forever Staff and Volunteers past and present. Furthermore, I'd like to give special gratitude of thanks to Bettie Murchison and Ursula Zeender-Tatro.

Acknowledgment

Archie Thornton Warren

I am his fourth child, and I am the person I am today because of him. Growing up in his household was no easy task; however, there was never any abuse, always plenty of food to eat and clean clothes to wear. Our family home, located on the outskirts of Benson, North Carolina, housed the nine of us.

As young as I can remember, my father always worked two jobs, which allowed my mother to be a stay-at-home mom. He was the primary breadwinner. He was truly the "Show and Tell" dad, meaning he SHOWED us what to do, then he TOLD us to go do. He only had a middle school education, and because he was the oldest, he had to drop out to help take care of his younger siblings. His firm belief in education persuaded my siblings and me to get a good education, which we all did. He was also a part of that education because, after each of his lectures (and they were many), his famous words were, "I'm not telling you what somebody told me, I'm telling you what I know." In other words, he was saying, "I learned this through the school of hard knocks."

He showed me what love and commitment was. He was married to his wife (our mom) for over 54 years and had a good relationship with his siblings and extended family. He was known in the community as a family man and a man of his word. He wasn't much of a churchgoer himself, but he made sure the Warrens were in church every Sunday. This occurred from as young as I can remember until I left to go to college.

No, he wasn't a perfect man, and there were times I thought his discipline was a bit harsh and sometimes painful, but I survived them, and I am a better person today because of it.

As I was putting the finishing touches on this book, a quote popped in my head, "Heaven must be like a father caring for the wellbeing of his children," if that's true, my mom, me, and my siblings witnessed Heaven in the house of Archie Warren. Rest in Peace, pops; this book is for you.

Your Son, Glenwood.

CONTENTS

About the Author

Glen Warren grew up in the countryside of Benson, North Carolina, where he and his siblings were given deep roots into the soil of their small family farm that brought forth food for nine people year after year after year. Most of the meat and vegetables every year were grown on that small farm of the Warren family. That upbringing prepared him and his siblings for adulthood, how to be responsible and how to take care of the families they would have one day. As each of Glen's siblings chose the path in life they wanted to live, Glen chose to be a social worker. Glen has a Bachelor of Science degree in Health and Physical Education from St Augustine's University. After getting a part-time job in the mental health field, his heart quickly left teaching gym classes in order to become a social worker.

After working in the field for over 25 years, Glen retired from Wake County Human Services in Raleigh, North Carolina. This retirement wasn't to travel and play with his grandchildren while sitting in his rocking chair, but to fulfill an assignment. This task was still in the people-helping business but by way of working with men, primarily fathers.

One Sunday afternoon, while standing in his living room with his three children, Glen explained to them, in words they could understand, that life as they knew it was about to change. That's the day Glen became a single father and the custodial parent to his three little ones, ages 7, 9, and 11. As Glen lay in bed that night pondering this unfamiliar territory, the thought hit him "I don't even know how to cook." One may ask, how could a 30 plus-year-old man never learned how to cook? You see, growing up on a small farm, learning how to cook wasn't a priority for his brothers and him. They worked along with his dad, mostly in the field, and his mom and sisters did most of the cooking and cleaning. When Glen graduated high school in May 1976, two months later, he was a student at St. Augustine's University and, for four years, had three meals a day prepared for him by the school's cafeteria.

During those summer months, Glen was back at home working in the field. His mom and his sisters still did the cooking; therefore, again, learning how to cook wasn't a priority. Glen graduated college in May 1980, and in July of the same year, he got married. For 15 years, the mother of his children was an excellent cook. She was also a stay-at-home mom, so again learning how to cook was not on Glen's list of chores to do, but things were about to change. Cooking now become a priority, and as a single parent of his three little ones, cooking was going to be a major part of his chores list. He had to learn how to cook and learn fast.

The first time he made spaghetti, he cooked the ground beef and boiled the noodles but what he didn't think to do, perhaps because he didn't know, was to drain the ground beef before adding the noodles. So, one can imagine what the outcome of that meal was. His daughter, at 7, said, "Daddy, we can't eat this." She asked, "Why didn't you drain the meat before you mixed it?" The answer was simple; Glen didn't know he was supposed to. At age 7, she probably knew more about cooking than he did. Glen guessed in her little mind, she thought, she had better learn how to cook; if not, they would all starve. They had a few more nights like that, but they survived, and Glen did manage to learn a little bit about cooking. In those early days, they ate a lot of already cooked fried chicken from Hardee's, KFC, Churches, and Bojangles. So much so that Glen's sons said they don't eat chicken even to this day because they ate more than their share growing up. (Not really, they still eat chicken. They just want to remind their dad of those many, many childhood chicken-eating days).

In 2008, Glen started Fathers Forever, a 501(3) nonprofit. The program serves as a map to help fathers chart a new course of fatherhood, as they are taught the vital role they play in their children's lives.

The goal is to promote responsible fatherhood. The program was designed and developed for non-custodial fathers who otherwise would go to jail for non-payment of child support. The fathers are ordered to attend the program's 12 weeks parenting classes where they are taught responsible fatherhood by using the curriculum the program created called "The Joys and Responsibilities of Fatherhood."

As mentioned before, Glen grew up in a loving home with his parents, who cared and provided for him and his siblings. Therefore, he knew what that feels like. That's a good feeling. For over 25 years, Glen worked with people with devastating childhoods, now suffering from Substance Abuse and Depression. A lot of them grew up in dysfunctional homes as they themselves were victims of abuse and broken childhoods. Glen had seen what that looks like, which was not pretty at all.

Being a single father and raising three children to adulthood, Glen knew the struggles that come with single parenting. He had been there, done that, and proudly wore that T-shirt. Nonetheless, he is still parenting because, on many levels, parenting never ends. Glen knew firsthand how important getting child support payments on time was as he did receive his child support payments timely which became a major part of his budget.

Many, many of Glen's clients over the years have sat weeping in his office as they remembered the pain from their childhood. Pain brought to them by the ones who said they loved them, the ones they called mommy and daddy. Glen's heart was saddened as he listened to those horror stories, but what could he do? How could he help heal these people who were hurting? He found a way through Fathers Forever to help parents not do to their sons and daughters what was done to them by their parents.

Preface

Separation may be hard for a couple, but for children, it can be the hardest. In most cases, children who come from divorced families are often, if not always, taken away from their fathers and compelled to stay with their mothers. But what happens when, and if, the roles are reversed? What if a father is provided with the opportunity to nurture his kids as their mothers would have? Would a father be able to carry out all the responsibilities with expertise that have traditionally been attached to the role of a mother?

I Am a Father Forever is a book about the many details regarding fatherhood that are often overlooked and are left unnoticed by the masses. I decided to write this book because I noticed that fatherhood is in crisis, and in order for men to become better fathers, someone had to take the first step. Being a single father and raising three children to adulthood myself, I am aware of the struggles a father is bound to undergo while bringing up his children singlehandedly.

Therefore, I truly believe it is essential for me to share the experiences that have helped me raise my kids and enable my fellow fathers to do the same skillfully. Moreover, I want to make them understand how this could lead to a fruitful bond that will bring lots of comfort and happiness, not just for themselves but for their little ones too.

Chapter 1

Statistics

When one who's fatherless chooses a life of crime, perhaps the runaway fathers should be charged with the crime of neglect.

Any man can have a child. That does not make you a father. It is the courage to raise a child that makes you a father. Beautiful words by Barrack Obama, the 44th President of the United States of America, explain the difference between a biological father and a father who nurtures a child. A father is responsible for taking care of their child as much as the mother. Any individual can join the army, but it takes a real soldier to hold his/her ground on the battlefield. Similarly, it is very easy to conceive a child, but playing a role in their life requires courage and strength.

Many societies have a culture where the fathers are responsible for earning the bread and butter for the family. At the same time, the mothers are expected to take care of the household and the kids' upbringing. It is important to note that it is not solely the mother's responsibility to nurture a child, and the reason is that children require the love and attention of both parents. If they lack that from any one of the parents, they could have mental health issues in their life. Research shows that developing a healthy relationship with both the parents is important. Likewise, it is not solely the responsibility of the father to be the earner unless some kind of arrangement is fixed between the parents. However, in my opinion, it is important to share all the responsibilities so that one parent does not end up blaming the other for everything.

No one can replace the role of a father. Studies have shown that if fathers are supportive and warm toward their children, it positively impacts the child's cognitive and social development. Many fathers find it convenient to leave their kids at an early age when the times get tough—not realizing how impactful that could be to their child's wellbeing. I always wonder how one can live with abandoning such a huge responsibility. How can someone's conscience allow that? However, many fathers out there simply do not care about the wellbeing of their children, which is extremely disappointing.

I am Glen Warren, the Founder and Executive Director of Fathers Forever, a nonprofit organization working to reduce the distance between fathers and their children, both physically and emotionally. Our vision is to 'serve children one father at a time,' i.e., reducing fatherless homes or homes where fathers are not as active in the relationship as required by a child's needs. We have been doing this through physical classes, virtual classes, as well as support groups. Additionally, we have an established educational institute called the Fathers Forever University, which is a twelve-week remote learning experience. Our classes help fathers with child support, anger management, parenting, co-parenting and substance abuse. Throughout this book, I will discuss similar topics, focusing on parenting, the importance of parenting, and issues associated with it. The latter topics will help me achieve my vision of making men better fathers.

I embarked on this journey because I had to face the struggles of being a single father myself, and that taught me, over time, how crucial and impactful parenting is for a child. When I had to cook for the first time for my kids (two sons and a daughter), I had no idea how to go about it. I realized that a simple task like cooking a meal for your child requires so much thought. For example, you have to take into account all that goes into a meal, making sure that the child's nutritional requirements are met. When we eat ourselves, we do not think as actively as to what we are consuming. However, for a child, especially when their growth is your responsibility, you have to take much more into consideration, like making sure they eat right and at the right time.

I also worked as a mental health counselor for over 20 years, helping disabled adults overcome issues in their lives. There, I worked with people coming from rough childhoods. Most of them suffered from substance abuse and depression, owing to dysfunctional homes and victims of bad parenting. The experiences I received there also reinforced the importance of parenting. Thus, after my retirement, I decided to help fathers become aware of the roles they were meant to play in their child's life. Since then, I can proudly say that I have impacted many lives and households through my program. Another proof of my accomplishments are my three children, all of whom have become great and successful adults.

There are countless statistics available on the internet that show how damaging it could be for children deprived of a healthy relationship with their fathers. Usually, I go through statistical figures in my classes and support programs to emphasize the importance of fatherhood. For example, a study conducted by the Center for Disease Control highlights that 85 percent of all children who show behavioral disorders come from fatherless homes. Behavioral disorders can seriously impact the child's ability to perform in schools and social settings, making life much more difficult than it should be. Since 85 percent of such children come from fatherless homes, just imagine how many children we could have saved from such disorders if only fathers played the role that was meant for them. Let's suppose that there are a thousand children with behavioral disorders. If only fatherless homes were resolved, only 150 out of the thousand kids would suffer from behavioral disorders. As you can see, fathers have such a huge impact on their children's lives; if only they understood. It would solve so many problems that exist in the world today.

Another study shows that 63 percent of teens who commit suicide are also from fatherless homes. That means more than half of teens who commit suicide are from fatherless homes, which only points out the magnitude of a father's role. Suicide is usually linked with mental disorders, which reiterates the significance of our previous statistics. A child without a father suffers from mental disorders initially and, due to those disorders, they are more likely to end up committing suicide. These statistics should help raise a father's conscience as his inability to successfully play his role can lead to the death of his child. I must ask again. How can someone's conscience allow that? A death caused by you will never allow you to sleep without guilt, and to avoid that from happening, one must think carefully about the role they play in their child's life.

The National Principals Association Report states that 71 percent of all high school dropouts come from fatherless homes. Again, as those children suffer from mental disorders that negate their educational and social ability, they find it extremely difficult to cope with their studies, make friends, deal with bullies, and so on. All this results in extreme frustration with academics and school life, leading the child to have no other option than to drop out for their wellbeing. Every parent wants their child to be happy and successful, but they do not realize how much effort it requires from their end, even more than the child himself. You cannot expect a flower to blossom unless you provide it with the right care. A flower does not blossom on its own, and neither does a child. However, the flower will blossom if you nurture it correctly, and so will the child!

Rainbow's for All God's Children is a support group for children who have suffered a significant loss in their lives. This organization has stated that 75 percent of all adolescent patients in chemical abuse centers come from fatherless homes. As most of us know, substance abuse can be caused by mental health disorders as it allows one to cope with their feelings more easily in the short run. However, substance abuse does not cure mental disorders. Rather, it makes these issues even worse as the person keeps trying to suppress them with different drugs. Substance dependency puts people in a vicious cycle as they keep using drugs to suppress their feelings. The problems keep getting worse, and, in turn, the person ends up taking more drugs. Drug addiction is a loop that eventually ends in disaster. Thus, fathers should realize that if they do not actively engage with their children, they may become a part of this loop and go as far as taking their own lives.

In September 1988, the United States Department of Justice concluded that 70 percent of youths in state-operated institutions come from fatherless homes—that is quite alarming! So, if a child does not commit suicide, there will be a high chance that they end up in a state-operated institution. The chances of a child functioning normally are going to be very low if the father fails to provide for him.

Many fathers do not realize the importance of giving to their children because they do not think of the day when they will require something from those very children. Obviously, you can take care of yourself in your thirties, forties, fifties, and sixties. What will you do when you are in a retirement home and your children do not even come to visit you? You may not need that emotional support now, but you will one day.

Another study conducted by the Center for Disease Control highlighted that 85 percent of all youth in prison come from fatherless homes. So, if fathers had played the role they were supposed to, there would only remain 15 percent of the youth in prison. I believe it is not entirely the kid's fault who ends up with criminal charges coming from a fatherless home. Their fathers should be held accountable as well. That is because the reason the child went down that path was the fault of the father as well. If a police officer catches someone consuming drugs, they always ask for the supplier as they are the ones who enabled the user in the first place. Likewise, fathers who abandon their children or do not play a sufficient role in their lives increase the probability of their child ending up homeless or even in jail!

A book titled 'Justice and Behavior' states that 80 percent of rapists with anger problems come from fatherless homes. This is a very unique and alarming statistic as children without fathers have not only a high tendency of becoming a rapist but also have anger problems alongside. This is not just alarming but extremely depressing as well. Rape culture is like a disease that has plagued our world for as long as one can remember. The fathers who fail to fulfill their roles are now playing a part in increasing the number of cases of these crimes. Not only have they destroyed their child's life, but they are now responsible for ruining the lives of all the victims as well. If their conscience was troubled before, now it must be a real mess. To all such fathers out there, please man up to your responsibilities. People blame governments for failed societies; I blame the people for not playing their part in society. Had they done that, the government could have focused on other things rather than fixing the mess the society has created.

One study has shown that 90 percent of all homeless and runaway children are from fatherless homes. Ninety percent! That is almost like saying all the homeless and runaway children are because of a lack of father figures in their lives. This statistic is pretty self-explanatory of the extent of the importance of fatherhood. Not growing under a father's shadow, a child has a high chance of facing mental disorders, suicide, substance abuse, a tendency for rape, juvenile delinquency, and so on. Now, we know how a child's future is affected if they grow up without a father, but do we know how much of a difference can be made in the world if fathers just played their parts? It is the choice of parents to bring a child into this world. The least they can do after that is to make sure that the child leads a healthy and happy life. You would never buy a car you would not drive, then why bring a child into this world that you will just abandon? A man's character is shown by the relationship he has with his family. Any man who can leave their family cannot be trusted as he lacks commitment, dedication, and loyalty. This is especially true for runaway fathers.

Reviewing the statistics we have discussed, it can be noticed that a child who lacks a father figure in his life has extremely low chances of being happy, healthy, normal, or successful. Rather, they are more likely to face jail time, substance abuse, crimes, suicidal thoughts, and mental disorders. Thus, if a man fails to be a 'right' father, he has ensured that his children will suffer for the rest of their lives.

I keep emphasizing on the fact that a person does not have to be absent from a child's life to cause all this trouble. Even if he does not nurture the child in a correct manner, that is almost the same as not being there. A person could actually cause more destruction by being there compared to not being there. I will explain throughout this book how parents can fail in parenting so that parents are much more aware and knowledgeable in conducting their daily lives.

In order to build on this point, I will discuss something that I call 'a fly on the wall' syndrome. Do you remember the times when you would be in another room but could hear your parents fight? How did that impact you as a kid? Did you ever witness any domestic violence at home? Did that build anger and hatred in you, maybe for a parent even? Scenarios like these are basically what I term as the 'fly on the wall' syndrome.

It means that an individual (in this case, your child) overhears a conversation that was not intended for them; additionally, the people conversing are not aware that someone is listening in on the conversation. Similar to a fly on the wall that we do not notice, but it is there, watching and listening to us.

Thus, when a parent speaks negatively about the other parent, the children listening are receiving information that they should not be receiving. Consequently, the children are making judgments about the parents without their knowledge. Sometimes, children overhear their parents conversing over the phone or with a guest. Now, they have to digest the fact that not just the parent, but also the relatives or whoever it is on the other end of the phone, think like that about the other

11

parent. How would something like that make you feel if your mom and your grandma are discussing how your father failed to provide for the family or that he is not man enough? Things like these can cause devastating impacts on children. We are teaching our children, by example, to dishonor/disrespect the other parent. They might end up having issues with authoritative figures like their parents, teachers, or even their supervisors at work.

Obviously, parents do not wake up thinking about insulting the other (some might!). Even if they do, I am sure that they do not intend for their children to find out— especially when parents get into fights and the name-calling starts. No parent wants their child to be exposed to the kind of language they use when they are fighting. Thus, all they need to do is to make efforts to make sure that they do not speak negatively about the other parent in front of their child. If they want to do it privately, they should make sure that the children are at a distance where they will not be able to overhear them. Such a small step for such a great impact. In my opinion, that is all that parenting requires. Taking baby steps to become more aware and knowledgeable about parenting as time goes by. Nobody expects a person to become a great parent overnight but taking the right steps in the right direction is a good start.

I have a friend who has an arrangement with his ex-wife which is that if any parent disrespects or says anything negative about the other parent, they have the right to sue the other. That, in my opinion, is a great step to becoming more conscious about what comes out of your mouth. The 'fly on the wall' syndrome can then be gotten rid of.

**

A note for parents: Do not abandon your children; they are your future and ours. Raise them the way you would want to be raised. Make them happy and successful. Always remember that their success and happiness will always be credited to you. Every child is known by their parents, and the way the kid turns out to be is the result of the parents' efforts. Do not blame the child for their failures as it is your failure, not theirs. They did not know better; you did. You could have taught them everything you think is important, but you had other priorities. So, just remember at all times, you have been given the opportunity of raising a child, a privilege that some parents do not even get. Make the most of that opportunity because if you destroy one child's life, you are destroying the lives of the many that are affected by them. Think about the impact your kid will eventually have on your grandkids. All I ask is for you to try to be better each day, even if it is a small thing like spending an extra five minutes with your child!

Now, just to make sure that you are reading and absorbing all the information I am trying to give you, I will be incorporating some questions at the end of each chapter. The answers will also be provided so that you can check your progress. I trust that you will not jump to the answers directly or look for them by going back to the chapter, even though you might be tempted to! Good luck! I hope you get all the answers correct because if you fail as a student, that means I failed as a teacher, just like the failure of a father from an unsuccessful child. If you do get some questions wrong, it is okay. That is the point of reading this book so that you can learn and grow. Hopefully, your progress will increase as you move on to the next chapters.

REVISION TIME!

Q. 1. Please fill out the blanks with the most appropriate answer from the brackets.

a) Society expects the _____ to be the bread earner of the family. (Father, Mother, Brother, Government)

b) ____ percent of all youth in prison come from fatherless homes. (51, 25, 85, 10, 100)

c) If a child is unsuccessful, it is the fault of their ____. (Siblings, Efforts, Teachers, Parents)

d) When cooking for your child, thinking about ____ is very important. (Money, Nutrition, Child Support, Expenses)

e) A child without a father has ____ chances of being successful. (Low, Mild, High, No)

Q. 2. Encircle 'True' or 'False' if you think the statements are right or wrong, respectively.

a) Sticks and stones may break bones, but words cannot hurt.

   True   False

b) A 'fly on the wall' is when kids overhear their parents speak nicely about them.

True   False

c) A child needs a father more than their mother.

True   False

d) 10 percent of all high school dropouts come from fatherless homes.

True   False

e) 63 percent of teens who commit suicide are from fatherless homes.

True   False

Q. 3. Describe in a single line what you have learned by reading this chapter.

_____

Answer Key

Q. 1. a) Society expects the <u>Father</u> to be the bread earner of the family.

Key note) This is just an expectation. The reality does not have to be that way. Additionally, all the responsibilities of a child are distributed evenly amongst both the parents. They can make their own arrangements, but both are held responsible for all aspects of their child's life.

b) <u>85 percent</u> of all youth in prison come from fatherless homes.

c) If a child is unsuccessful, it is the fault of their <u>parents</u>.

Key note) Other factors also go in to your child's upbringing, such as friends and schooling, so it is possible that you did everything that you could, but your child still suffers from mental health issues. However, if you have done your part, at least you will not be living with the guilt of not fulfilling your responsibility.

d) When cooking for your child, thinking about <u>nutrition</u> is very important.

Key note) Thinking about money and expenses is also important; however, priority should be given to your child's nutritional needs over finances.

e) A child without a father has <u>low</u> chances of being successful.

Q. 2. a) False. Words can hurt just as much, if not more, as physical pain. A 'fly on the wall' is a good example of that.

b) False. A 'fly on the wall' represents kids hearing a parent talk negatively about the other, without the parents' knowledge that the conversation is being heard.

c) False. A child needs both their mother and father, equally.

d) False. 71 percent of all high school dropouts come from fatherless homes.

e) True.

Q. 3. There is no right answer for this. As long as you have an answer to this question, that is all that matters. I want you to takeaway something from each chapter, and this answer highlights that takeaway. If you do not have an answer, reread the chapter and try to take a lesson from it.

Chapter 2

Legacy

Parent's relationship with each other can forever affect their child's wellbeing.

"What you leave behind is not what is engraved in stone mountains, but what is woven into the lives of others," said Pericles, a Greek statesman and General of Athens during the golden age. The quote captures the essence of the term 'legacy.' If you think about the word's literal meaning, it merely means the money or properties that you leave behind, kind of like inheritance that you pass on. However, the 'legacy' that we will be talking about in this book is not limited to that definition. Instead, we will focus on legacy as what you leave behind for your children, which encompasses everything, not just the material things.

Pericles describes this notion perfectly as he terms legacy as something that is engraved into the lives of others. That could be the values, ethics, life lessons, attitudes, and so much more. Your duty as a father does not end when you pass away; it actually transcends your death. Your legacy is lived by your children in a way. If you taught them to be nice to others without any motive and they keep following that advice after your death, your children are carrying on your legacy, i.e., your duty as a father is in motion even after your death.

Thus, anything and everything that you pass on to your children, relatives, and friends should be well thought of as it will define who you were as a person. The way your child turns out to be is a reflection of how you raised them. If you pass down the right things, your child will turn out to be good and vice versa. To make sure that your legacy is positive, you have to ensure that you live and preach that positivity.

The fathers in my program are always coming up to me to ask what they should be leaving behind for their children. Usually, they believe that they are responsible for leaving them enough money or properties so that their children do not struggle much in life. However, I think that this approach is not holistic. You can leave your children all the money, cars, and properties, but if they are not taught how to use that money, then they can easily lose it all in a couple of years. What will your children do then? Have you taught them the importance of money and how to utilize it?

These kinds of questions turn your attention toward

what you have taught your child. In my opinion, that matters much more than any materialistic possessions. They can earn more money, buy more cars and be much more successful if you teach them how to achieve things in life rather than just handing it to them on a silver platter.

I know it is difficult, extremely difficult for some, to focus on something other than making money these days. Times go by much faster, the competition has increased immensely, and we are all occupied with making sure that we have enough food on the table and enough money to pay the rent. However, even if you spend 12 hours a day at work, I will not ask you to cut down on your work hours to spend more time with your children. I know you are not working those 12 hours out of joy; I know it is a necessity rather than a choice. All I want from you is to take out just an hour for them, if that is too much, take out half an hour. Make sure to spend a little time with your kids, teaching them about life and how to approach it. If you are struggling in life, share those experiences with your children. They will appreciate your struggle more than the stressed version they see of you, which does not make any sense to them as they are not aware of what is going on around them.

Some of the parents are not even aware of what they

are leaving behind for their children. When I talk to them about this, they tell me that they have never even thought about this, which surprises me a lot. Have you actively thought about how you are building your legacy, especially for your children? Have you thought about what values you want to leave them with? If not, you should start actively thinking about it. Teach your children the difference between right and wrong. Bring them toward spirituality so that they can better themselves. Invest in their education so they can build their own empires instead of you making it for them. Teach them how to face the difficulties of life with a smile on their faces. Teach them to love, forgive and give to charity.

If you ask your children, now, what should be left for them, they might gravitate toward the material things. They might even despise you for focusing on values and ethics rather than buying them the new Corvette. However, when they grow up and mature, they will definitely thank you for all that you have done. They will appreciate the things that you left behind because it still helps them. The money that you leave can be erased within a couple of years, after which the same children who wanted that expensive car will blame you for not leaving enough. On the other hand, the kid who is facing stress at work will always be thankful to you for teaching them how to deal with stress.

You should not focus on what your kids want but rather on what they will need when you are gone. I will discuss some myths and facts pertaining to what children expect from their fathers. Let's see if you can tell if these statements are a myth or fact.

Fatherhood begins for a man the moment the child is born. Even though this statement might seem very true, it is actually a myth. Fatherhood actually begins when the child is conceived. Your role as a father is to take care of the mother of your child, make sure she eats the right things and does not overburden herself with anything. That will result in a healthier baby, who will be better able to carry on your legacy in the future.

Fathers are better than mothers at disciplining their children. This is not true either. Fathers are much stricter when it comes to disciplining the child. They tend to take a bossy role versus the mother, who actually acts like a leader. This does not have to be the case in every household, but it is more likely to happen. Mothers usually use the father as threats; for example, we have all heard the following, "Don't make me call your dad!" Fathers are gravitated toward punishments, while mothers have a more loving and forgiving nature. Thus, if you want that positive legacy, leave the disciplining to your better half.

Fathers are as sensitive to their infants as mothers. This may seem untrue, given mothers are more loving and caring, but fathers are actually very good at understanding their child's needs. Fathers can differentiate when their babies are crying because of hunger, injury, or frustration. Since they are so responsive to their children, it allows them to understand how the child feels. Moreover, if you are sensitive toward your children, then you will have a healthier relationship with them, allowing you to pass on the right things to your children.

Children seem to prefer their fathers as play partners. This is a fact because, usually, fathers spend more time playing with the kids than mothers. The mothers are usually busy doing household chores and are not as excited to play as fathers. Fathers are usually geared toward physical activities, and so the children can easily pick up their playful nature. You would expect a father to wrestle with their children, and even though the mothers can do it too, they usually prefer not to. It is important for fathers to be playful with their kids in order for the kids to do the same for the next generation. Your legacy, in this case, would be passing down your playful nature.

When non-resident fathers pay child support, their

children are more likely to be healthy. This is true because this allows the mothers to take care of their child's nutrition, health, education and other needs. If you don't pay child support and the mother cannot afford to provide for the child's needs, then how will he/she remain healthy? Additionally, you will be passing down your responsible nature.

Inner-city children who receive child support from their fathers are just as likely to live in poverty as those who don't. This is clearly a myth as it builds on the previous point. If you give your children hospital access, education and good nutrition, their chances of success have already improved immensely!

Fathers have their greatest influence on their sons when they are teenagers. This is a myth because the most influence you have over your children is when they are in early childhood. That is the phase when they are learning the most and you should be there to teach them the right things. When fathers are absent, there is a greater likelihood that their sons will be violent. Boys who lack a caring male role model have a stronger need to prove their masculinity.

A father's relationship with the mother of his child does not necessarily influence how his child views him. That is the first relationship a child observes and learns the most from. It will influence the child's image of you, as well as the mother. Remember, sometimes, you don't even have to teach something for them to learn. Children are very good observers, so if you have a bad relationship with their mother, it can easily influence how your child will behave with their partner.

The quality of time a father spends with his child is more important than the length of time. This is true, and I have explained this before as well. Even if you take out half an hour from your day to spend with your kids, make sure it is productive. Teach them the things you want them to remember for the rest of their lives. Bear in mind, quality over quantity.

There are around 70 million men that identify as being a father in the United States. However, only less than half of those have a home where they are with a spouse and children under the age of 18, which means that in the remaining (more than half) homes, the kids are being raised without either parent. Children that are raised by a single parent or without parents have way fewer chances of being healthy or successful compared to the children that have both their parents.

The statistics we discussed in the previous chapter showed how important it is for the child to have a father at home, and we will be building more on that case.

Additionally, we should try to focus on having both the parents at home since it is equally important for the mother to have an active role as well. The reason why I emphasize the fathers is that they are more likely to walk away from their responsibility.

A study by the National Public Radio shows us some very interesting statistics. For example, girls, who come from fatherless homes, have a hundred percent higher risk of suffering from obesity compared to girls who have their fathers. Furthermore, girls without fathers are four times more likely to become pregnant before reaching the age of 20. How do you expect to pass down any sort of legacy when you are absent from the lives of the people who actually matter?

A very interesting study by the U.S. Department of Health and Human Services shows that given the same financial condition, children who come from homes that have both parents outperform children that have a single parent. Obviously, if two people are there to take care of you, they have higher chances of success than a single parent because they have to do everything on their own.

Child support can be a really strong tool to help out single parents who are struggling for their children's sake. It allows the mothers to focus on their child's needs, such as their health, education and wellbeing. If the mother has the responsibility of the finances as well, then how will she do the other things?

As a father, if you cannot stay in the house, even though we have discussed how important it is for a father to play an active role in their child's life, you should at least pay child support. No matter how much you dislike the mother, your child did not do anything for you to lash the anger toward the whole house. Rather, you should separate from the mother, pay child support to ensure all your child's needs are met and spend time with them to teach them the important aspects of life. Do everything that you can so that your legacy is reflected in your children and the generations to come after.

Unfortunately, some kids are not even aware of who their biological father is, and therefore, establishing paternity is essential. Paternity establishes a legal relationship between a father and his children, even if they are adopted. It establishes the rights and obligations that both parties hold for each other. Claiming paternity is also important to settle things like divorce, child custody and child support.

If the parents of a child are not married or there is doubt about who the real father is, paternity must be established to clear all the confusions. Even if you are under

18, you can declare paternity. If you think you are the father of a child, but the mother does not think so, you can even ask for a blood test. These blood tests are nearly a hundred percent accurate in telling who the father is.

Furthermore, if you pay child support on time, the government adds a little bonus to the support that is given to the mother. Thus, no matter what your excuses are, there is none for doing the bare minimum. You are only liable to pay until the child turns 18; after that, you have no such responsibilities. Therefore, fathers should pay the child support through these years wholeheartedly.

Due to the abnormality of the absence of fathers, some little boys have been deprived of life's lessons regarding how to be a good man. Yet, they are told, "Go be a man." I will share a story with you that explains how some fathers make excuses to not support their children due to the toxic relationship they have had with the mother. The story is titled "Dead or Alive: Which is it?"

A father we will call Ken was ordered to attend Fathers Forever classes. He was a very outgoing guy and was the life of the party wherever he went. He was very friendly, and I could tell after a couple of classes that he was probably a hell-raiser in his younger days. I soon found how right I was.

29

About two months after Ken had started our classes, we had a graduation for another group of guys who had completed the program's requirements. Ken was also invited to this event. He was very touched by the ceremony, and he cheered the guys on as they received their certificates. A friend of mine who attended the graduation knew Ken. This friend called me later to tell me about his experience with him, which was not at all good. He told me, "He is a good guy, but he has a lot of issues." My friend went on to say, "If you can get to this guy, I will tip my hat to you."

As the classes went on, I began to get a better understanding of what my friend meant about Ken. He complained a lot about the system and about the mother of his child. Often during class, I had to redirect him to give the other guys the opportunity to share their stories or comments.

In our 12-week class curriculum, there are eight modules of three classes each. One module is called "Let It Go." In these three classes, we deal with unforgiveness, bitterness, and resentment. As we started the first class on forgiveness, I shared with the participants that forgiveness and unforgiveness are both a person's choice. Ken sat very quietly; I didn't have to redirect him even once during this class. I thought maybe he wasn't feeling well, so after class, I asked him if everything was okay. He replied yes; he was good. But there was something about the way he said "yes" that cast some doubt in my mind. I couldn't put my finger on it, so I let it go and decided not to push it.

During the next class, we talked about bitterness, if left unresolved, it can cause anger, malice, resentment, and sometimes, even hatred. Ken sat quietly; again, not one time did I have to redirect him. However, during the class, I began to pay a little more attention to his body language. He was very attentive, but he wouldn't make eye contact with me. I knew then that he was listening and maybe struggling with what I was saying, though, apparently, not in a bad way. We talked briefly after class. He seemed to be a little more talkative but still was not the outspoken guy who took over the conversations like he had been in the past few weeks.

In the next class, we talked about resentment and that resentment and bitterness are two sides of the same coin: they are both passive-aggressive reactions to anger. Resentment is the attitude of displeasure, cynicism, and hostility a person has toward someone. Bitterness is a grievous and distressful inner feeling. During that class, I also shared a story called "Crazy Like a Fox," subtitled "The Blame Game." Perhaps that story gave Ken his breakthrough.

The phrase "crazy like a fox" is misleading because the nature of a fox is not really insanity; rather, a fox operates in cunning and deceit. The term is used when one appears to be crazy but is acting with hidden motives while functioning in a cunning way, as a fox does. I will paraphrase the story here, but you can read it in its entirety in my first book, Chat and Chew.

When things happen to us, there is a space between what happened and our response to it. In that space, we are responsible for our decisions, reactions, and behavior. We can choose to grow and mature in that space, and it will be reflected in our reactions and behavior, or we can allow our growth to be stunted in that space. That decision, too, will be reflected in our reactions and behavior. So, I asked them this question as I walked slowly toward Ken "How do you respond when life happens? Remember, your response will be reflected in your behavior."

I gave them some examples; it's true: your Daddy wasn't present in your life, but how long are you going to use his absence as your excuse for not taking care of your children? It's true: your old man did leave you and the children for another woman, but how long are you going to blame him for that space of bitterness in which you have chosen to remain? It's a fact: you did grow up on the wrong side of the tracks. But at some point, you have to stop living in that space of blaming the system for your victim mentality. And yes, it's a fact: someone mishandled you and hurt you down to your core, but how long will you walk in that space of unforgiveness?

We have to stop blaming others for the decisions we make. The blame game doesn't work. We must all make the choice to grow and not be stunted in our spaces of limitation. The word "stunt" means to stop, slow down, or hinder growth or development. I concluded with this statement: "It's easy to blame others, and it may be difficult to stop blaming others, but WE must stop." As I was speaking, I was looking straight into Ken's eyes, he didn't look away this time, but he had a slight grin on his face as to say, you got me. All three of these classes were hitting Ken right where he lived.

He later told me that the class on forgiveness started him on the road to attitude healing.

Here is where the title of this story, "Dead or Alive," came from. In a previous relationship, Ken fathered a child, and a few years later, he and the child's mother discontinued their relationship. They both moved on. Years passed, and neither one reached out to the other one.

Ken later found out the mother told their child that he was deceased. Of course, Ken was furious that the mother had lied to their child and put all the blame on her for keeping his child away from him. He said he vowed in his heart never to forgive her for that deception.

As he told the story, I could see on his face and hear in his voice the anger, the bitterness, and the resentment he had toward his child's mother. He had lived with those feeling for years. He declared that she had done a very hateful thing. I could also hear the hurt and sadness in his voice. I didn't confront him that day because he wasn't in a place to hear what I had to say, but I got a chance to do it a few weeks later.

One day, Ken and I met again after class, and this time I did confront him with a question —actually three questions: You did know you weren't dead, right? You did know you had a child, right? When he answered yes to both questions, I asked the third question: why didn't you try to find out where your child was? After a pause — he didn't really have a good answer — he came up with a few excuses like I was young; I wasn't ready to be a father; I had a lot of other issues going on.

Then he said, as he was looking away, "After I found out she said I was dead, I was hurt and angry and said to myself, 'forget it.' I knew I didn't have myself together, so I thought the child would be better off without me. But then (I could hear his anger surging), I was hit with child support. Mr. G., why am I paying for a child I can't see and don't have a relationship with?" I responded, "Because he's your child and part of the reason you don't have a relationship with the child is because of your own choosing."

I could see that he wanted to blame the mother again, but he caught himself and said, "These classes have helped me a lot, and now I know what I have to do. I have to let this bitterness and resentment go, forgive her, and try to build a relationship with my son." He then said, "You have a way with words Mr. Glen. That crazy-like-a-fox story really hit home."

He later graduated from class and was one of the fathers who shared their stories. He said, "I now have a relationship with my child. It's not a really good one yet, but we are working on it." He also said, "I'm trying to improve my relationship with my son's mother as well. It's hard. For so many years, I blamed her, but I realize now I have to blame myself as well. I have to move past what she did to help create a better relationship with my child."

Ken's speech brought the audience to tears, and they

gave him a much-deserved standing ovation.

My friend who had spoken to me about Ken early on was there, and as he had promised, he did tip his hat to me.

Thus, no matter what your reason is for not being there, it is not the child's fault. Do you want to leave behind a legacy of being the absent one or the one who fought for his kids? The one who overcame all obstacles to fulfill their child's needs? If you ask me, I would rather have the latter.

I AM A FATHER FOREVER

REVISION TIME!

Q. 1. Please fill out the blanks with the most appropriate answer from the brackets.

a) Fatherhood begins for a man the moment the child is ____. (born, conceived, breathing, talking)

b) You are only liable until the children are ____. (16, 20, old, teenagers, 18)

c) Paternity establishes a ____ relationship between a father and his children. (bonding, healthy, legal, loving, serious)

d) Children seem to prefer their ____ as play partners. (father, mother, grandfather, grandmother)

e) Children who come from homes that have both parents ____ children that have a single parent. (underperform, love, outperform, hit)

Q. 2. Encircle 'True' or 'False' if you think the statements are right or wrong, respectively.

a) Due to the abnormality of the absence of fathers, some little boys have been deprived of life's lessons regarding how to be a man.

True   False

b) When fathers are absent, there is a lesser risk that their sons will be violent.

True   False

c) The quality of time a father spends with his child is more important than the length of time.

True   False

d) Child support can be a weakness of the single parent.

True   False

e) When non-resident fathers pay child support, their children are more likely to be healthy.

True   False

Q. 3. Describe in a single line what you have learned by reading this chapter.

_____

I AM A FATHER FOREVER

Answer Key

Q. 1. a) Fatherhood begins for a man the moment the child is conceived.

b) You are only liable until the children are 18.

c) Paternity establishes a legal relationship between a father and his children.

d) Children seem to prefer their father as play partners.

e) Children who come from homes that have both parents outperform children that have a single parent.

Q. 2. a) True.

b) False.

c) True.

d) False.

e) True.

Q. 3. If you do not have an answer, reread the chapter and try to take a lesson from it. There is no right or wrong answer for this.

Chapter 3

Budget

Being a Dad is a matter of choice, then obligation.

"Don't tell me what you value, show me your budget, and I'll tell you what you value," said Joe Biden, the 46th (and current) President of the United States of America. The President tries to explain, with this statement, that the money you spend reflects who you are as a person. Your budget (or the way you spend) defines what and who you really care about. You spend on the things that matter the most to you. Thus, if you are spending more on yourself than others, you probably care about yourself the most.

How much of your budget is allocated toward your family? Is it enough to satisfy their needs and wants? If not, you should rethink the way you spend because your children are entitled to your money. They did not have a choice for coming into this world, you did. Now that they are here, make sure to give them enough to satisfy their basic needs. For you, it is not a matter of choice but an obligation.

Some people prefer spending on luxuries while others focus on their savings. Savings are essential for the long run; you never know when you might need the extra money. You never know when that hospital expenditure or the child support payments that you have been trying to get away with might hit you. However, if you set the right budget, you should not have to worry about future costs. Budgeting allows you to plan for the future while making sure that you are allocating enough for your current needs.

Another important factor to consider while creating a budget is any child support payment. As discussed before, even if you do not like the mother, or cannot visit your child, you are still obliged to pay child support for bringing a life into this world. It is crucial to make these payments on time to ensure that your child's needs are met on time. Furthermore, you should also be aware of how those payments are being spent. If you are unaware of child support or its processes, I will be explaining the concept here in this chapter in detail.

Child support, in its legal definition, is an ongoing payment that you have to make periodically. It is made by a parent to support the financial needs of their child or the mother. Child support is usually established at the end of a relationship, which could be a breakup or divorce. There could be a case where the mother of the child does not have a job, so in order to raise the child, these support payments will help take care of not only the child but the mother as well. If your child is in a state-owned facility, your payments will be supporting the state. Basically, the obligor has to pay to the obligee. The obligor is not necessarily the father, it depends on who is taking custody of the child and who earns more income. Thus, the mother could also be the obligor, depending on the circumstances.

Custody of the child is one of the most important elements in child support. It is a legal term, which establishes the guardian of the child, i.e., the custodian. There are two types of custody, legal and physical. Legal custody establishes the right to make decisions regarding the child's life, while physical custody refers to the obligation to provide a house, food and other needs.

A lot of fathers have come up to me with complaints regarding how their child support money is being spent on things like the mother's hair, nails and so on. They are worried that the mothers are exploiting the money for their personal gains instead of using it on the child.

I will tell you my personal story, which will help you understand how to deal with the above-mentioned issues and give you an idea of how the child support money gets spent. I have two sons and a daughter and I am a single parent, as I have mentioned before. I want to show you how I budgeted my income and how I used the child support money. At the time when I was raising my kids, my salary per year was $34,000, out of which $2,800 was taken as taxes. My monthly income came out to be $2,123, which is not a lot of money. I was unable to work two jobs as I had to take care of the kids because they were quite young at the time. However, I did get child support payments which were $352. Thus, the total monthly income was around $2,495. Whenever I got paid, I made sure to pay all my bills because then I would have to wait another 30 days to get my salary.

Therefore, I really needed to budget my money, and I could not have survived without the help of my family and church members. It's very easy to think that your money is being misused, but that's the picture you get from the outside. If you dwell on the internal financial situation, it will change your perspective about the money being wasted. I will share my expenses with you to give you an idea of how a household with children runs financially.

To run a household, you need to have multiple basic things like food, water, lighting and heat. I know a lot of households that have been evicted or had their utilities cut off due to non-payment. Some of you might have experienced something similar as well, where you might have had to survive on canned foods due to a low budget. I have faced issues like that in the past too. For example, there was a month when my car broke down, and this unexpected expense hindered my ability to pay all the bills. Therefore, I was unable to pay the water bill, and the company came and cut off my water supply as well as the meter associated with it. I had to pay the water bill and the meter, which was $150. This happened a couple of times, and it upset my budget for other expenses.

Things like this can happen to anyone, and therefore, financial support becomes crucially important. Some of you have probably suffered from your car being repossessed or your phone cut off because of non-payment. I have had my car taken away as I did not have enough money to make the installment payments. Whenever you struggled to make payments on time, you probably had to deal with people who were extremely rude by the way they talk, as they do not understand what you are going through. They are only concerned about their payments. The guy who was supposed to take my car did the same thing. He tried to force me to pay by shouting abuses and being extremely rude, but that is something you just have to deal with at the time. I even tried to hide my car from the repo man, but he still found it!

The point is, you have to make payments every thirty days, and if you miss a cycle, something is definitely getting cut off! Thus, you have to ensure that you are financially supporting your family so that they do not have to go through all this.

I will describe my expenses as well to show you how the money gets spent. I had to pay $700 per month for rent, $350 for my mobile home, of three bedrooms, and $350 for the lot rent. That was a significant amount of money just for rent, which was almost thirty percent of my whole income! The electricity bill would come out to $125 on average. Then we had the expenses for food, which was around $400 for three children and myself. This was a fairly low budget, but it was enough to keep 'decent enough' food on the table. The water bill would be around $60 since I had a washing machine at home. I also had two phone lines, one for the house and one for work. Two phones were essential to keep in touch with my children at all times. The bill for the two phones was around $100. My car payment each month was $325 for my Honda Accord and $110 for insurance. If you miss any of these payments, then you have to pay the penalties as well! Further,

I spent $200 on gas and clothing. Then there are the expenses of going out, or your kids need something for school. These expenses vary a lot and depend on the month's situation. There could be a birthday or a new video game coming out, and so, for miscellaneous expenses, I would keep $300.

Overall, the budget is quite conservative and sticks to the basic necessities only. If you calculate the total income minus the total expenses, the remaining balance for the month comes out to be around $240. If I had not received any child support, I would be standing at a negative balance of $112. Now, some people assume that child support money is being spent on personal luxuries. However, I have shown you the reality of budgeting and the expenses. If you decide to stop paying those child support payments, people like me will end up with a negative balance. What does negative balance mean? It means something is going to get cut off, be it the light or gas. One might even get evicted.

Therefore, we have to understand what actually is important. We have to set our priorities straight. Let's say you saved the $350 that you were supposed to pay for your child support. What are you going to do with that money? You might spend it on some new clothes or hangouts with your friends. What is the opportunity cost? Your family suffers to pay for their needs, has to argue with the possessors and might even face eviction! Is an expensive dinner with your friends more important than the shelter over your kids' heads?

I was making $2,123 a month at work. Let's say the people at my company pay me for 32 hours a week instead of the 40, which they might term as loss in production. That will upset my budget drastically; I might not be able to meet ends with that money. Thus, financial support, as stated multiple times before, cannot be taken lightly at all. The best thing that I had going on was the support of my ex-wife, who paid all her child support payments on time. If she had not, I do not know where I would have been today, or even my kids, for that matter. Remember, my family members had to pitch in as well. Thus, you can clearly see how difficult it is to raise a family alone. Please make sure to make your payments on time so that the difficulties do not increase on them.

Do not assume that the other person is wasting your money on unnecessary things; even if they are spending a little on themselves, they deserve that. They are busy working and taking care of the child. On top of that, they do not have any money to spend on themselves. However, if they manage to spare a few bucks for a new pair of sneakers that they desperately required, give them a little break. Otherwise, step up and own your responsibilities, take care of your child. You can ask the mother that you will be paying the rent if you think they might waste the money. Instead of focusing on the excuses of getting out of payments, fathers should be focusing on the solutions for their children. Try to do one thing, be empathetic. Try to understand why the mother needs those payments and the impact that a mere $350 has on the whole household. If you cannot do it for the mother's sake, do it for the children.

Remember, fathers, you are responsible for all of your children: Those you live with and those you deny. I say this quite often.

Most of the time, the father's ego comes in between them and their child. For example, they had a fight with their wife, which ended in a divorce. They are so angry with their wives that they end up ignoring their children. That should not be the case. Your relationship with your child is separate from the relationship you had with your wife. Do not let pitiful things such as ego hold you back from fulfilling your responsibilities. I will share a story that highlights this case quite well; it is called 'Rumor has it.'

The word on the street, also known as a rumor, means a story or statement in general circulation without confirmation or facts; however, sometimes, the facts eventually come out. It may take a while —months, even years — but the truth eventually comes out for all to see.

In this case, a girl meets a boy, and there is a physical attraction for both of them. They exchange contact information, and a short time later, after they contact each other, they get together. In a "one-night stand," the girl gets pregnant. Some people have one-night stands often, and I guess it works for them. But things can really get complicated when a precious life is created in a one-night stand. So, it was in this case.

Let me set the stage. This father — let's call him Frank (the name has been changed to protect the guilty) — was ordered by Wake County Child Support Enforcement Office to attend Fathers Forever Parenting Class. The program serves as a map to help fathers chart a new course of fatherhood. Our program is designed and developed for non-custodial fathers who otherwise would go to jail for non-payment of child support. They are ordered to attend one of the two classes offered weekly). Frank already had a seven-year-old son whom he saw almost every day. He had a great relationship with his son and his son's mother even though the two weren't a couple anymore. Frank also had a five-year-old daughter he

49

had never seen before, and it was her case that got him ordered to attend Fathers Forever.

Frank's five-year-old daughter was the child of another young lady he was dating. When she got pregnant, he told her he wasn't ready to be a father again and wanted her to have an abortion. When she refused, he ended the relationship and told her she was on her own, and he wasn't going to support her or the child. She moved back home to be with her family, and a few months later, Frank's little girl was born. Rumor had it (the word in the street) that Frank had fathered another child, but of course, he denied it.

After a few more years went by, the rumor made its way to the child support enforcement office. Then one day, Frank received a letter requesting a blood test. When the results came back, the rumor was confirmed as fact: Frank had another child.

In Fathers Forever classes, Frank often said he wasn't ready for another child, and he claimed he told the mother that, but she didn't consider what he wanted. He stated, "She wanted to have the child; I didn't want another child. I guess my decision didn't matter." He said he felt like he had no choice in the matter. He was very angry and resentful toward the mother and even toward his daughter, who he had never seen.

My challenge to Frank was that he did have a choice, and he did choose. He looked at me with confusion and anger. Then I made this statement to him, and he got it, or at least I thought he got it: "You did make a choice. The choice was to have unprotected sex, and she made the same choice." Then I said, "She embraced and has been living with her decision over the past few years. You have been running from your decision over the past few years."

He looked like he had been hit with a ton of bricks. He said, "I never thought about it quite like that."

Over the course of our weekly classes, Frank embraced his daughter, accepted her, and started paying his child support. He is now living happily as a responsible father to her and to his son. Frank had two children and is now taking care of both of them. By this time, Frank was involved in another relationship, and wedding bells were ringing. But there is another chapter in Frank's story: "The One-Night Stand."

As I mentioned earlier, a girl meets a boy, and their physical attraction leads to pregnancy. Thus, the simplicity of a one-night stand gets really complicated. This is a bombshell for Frank, who has been down this road before. Frank apparently hasn't learned much, however. As I wrote earlier, I thought he got it before but apparently not. Frank took a page from his old playbook and tried to solve the same problem the same way he did before with yet another woman. He told her he wasn't ready to be a father again and wanted her to have an abortion. When she refused, he ended all contact with her.

Frank was very angry and resentful toward yet another mother. He changed his telephone number to avoid any contact from her. Now, here comes another bombshell: Frank learns the woman he is about to marry is pregnant as well. The babies are born only three months apart. Frank lives with one mother and his child, but he has no contact with the other mother or the child, just like before. But the word in the street — rumor — is that Frank has another child. Of course, he denies it, but again the rumor made its way to the child support enforcement office, and once again, Frank gets a letter, takes the blood test, and another rumor is confirmed as fact: Frank has fathered another child.

Frank has four children now: two of them were born in the same year, only a few months apart. He has a good relationship with three of them, but one of them — an adorable five-year-old boy —he has never laid eyes on. This loving, handsome, and very smart little boy has a loving family on his mother's side and plenty of father figures, aunts, uncles, cousins, and two grandparents who would lay down their lives for him. The only thing the child is lacking is the voice and support of his father. Sometimes the child asks, "Where is my daddy?" Frank pays his child support but hasn't found the courage to fight through the things that keep him from his son.

What is it with Frank and the many men like him — the one-night standers? Maybe their love is not enough to include all of their children.

Fathers, will you gather all of your children under your wings? You are responsible for all of your children: those you live with and those you deny or have never seen before because the word on the street or the rumor has it that you have fathered other children. Perhaps one day, those rumors will be confirmed.

REVISION TIME!

Q. 1. Please fill out the blanks with the most appropriate answer from the brackets.

a) _____ are essential for the long run. (Parties, Savings, Phones, Houses)

b) _____, in its legal definition, is an ongoing payment that you have to make periodically. (Custody, Paternity, Child support, Custodian)

c) _____ allows you to plan for the future while making sure that you are allocating enough for your current needs. (Marriage, Planning, Budgeting, Analysis)

d) The word on the street, also known as a _____, means a story or statement in general circulation without confirmation or facts. (lie, fact, dream, drama, rumor)

e) Child support is usually established at the end of a _____. (contract, procedure, relationship, crime, friendship)

Q. 2. Encircle 'True' or 'False' if you think the statements are right or wrong, respectively.

a) Custody of the child is one of the most important elements in child support.

    True   False

b) Do assume that the other person is wasting your money on unnecessary things.

    True   False

c) Most of the time, the father's ego helps the relationship with their child.

    True   False

d) Child support can be a weakness for the custodian as it may lead to laziness.

    True   False

e) An important factor while creating a budget is any expense for partying.

    True   False

Q. 3. Describe in a single line what you have learned by reading this chapter.

_____

Q. 4. Describe in a single line how you will be applying what you have learned in this chapter.

_____

Answer Key

Q. 1. a) <u>Savings</u> are essential for the long run.

b) <u>Child support</u>, in its legal definition, is an ongoing payment that you have to make periodically.

c) <u>Budgeting</u> allows you to plan for the future while making sure that you are allocating enough for your current needs.

d) The word on the street, also known as a <u>rumor</u>, means a story or statement in general circulation without confirmation or facts.

e) Child support is usually established at the end of a <u>relationship</u>.

Q. 2. a) True.

b) False.

c) False.

d) False.

e) False.

Q. 3 & 4. If you do not have an answer, reread the chapter and try to take a lesson from it. There is no right or wrong answer for these.

Chapter 4

Parenting

Co-Parenting is focusing on your children, not each other.

"It is easier to build strong children than to repair broken men," as said by Frederick Douglas, a prominent activist, author and public speaker. This explains what we have been discussing thus far. It is important to build the foundation of the building in order for it to soar high in the sky. The same applies to the people in our societies; if they are taught and raised well, nobody can stop them from reaching heights of success. Frederick Douglas's words convey that it is much easier to raise children the right way, allowing them to be better people in the future, compared to trying to fix the faults in society present today. The adults of the future can fix those faults if you raise them the right way.

Parenting refers to the promotion and support of your child's physical, emotional and social development. It is more about the act of parenthood rather than the biological relationship of the parents. As discussed before, birthing a child does not make you a father but spending time with them and raising them is what being a father actually means. In some cases, parenting is done by people who are not the biological parents, for example, an older sibling, a grandparent, a step-parent, any legal guardian, a relative, a family friend or even the government. No matter who the parents are, a very important factor in parenting is co-parenting.

Co-parenting is the act of sharing the responsibilities of parenthood. It becomes extremely important after a divorce as it allows both the parents to continue supporting their children as a team. Being a team requires both the partners to be in constant communication as well as respect for the other co-parent. Any parent, be it mother or father, who fails to follow these guidelines, will fail in being a good co-parent. Always remember that your priority is your children, so any sacrifices you make for your partner are, in fact, for your kids. As discussed multiple times before, having both parents for a child is very crucial in their development and wellbeing. Thus, even if you dislike your partner, just stick in there for the kids' sake. Heather Hetchler, an author, describes co-parenting perfectly, "Co-parenting. It's not a competition between two homes. It's a collaboration of parents doing what is best for the kids."

I like using the term co-pilot instead of co-parent as it embraces the same nature of the job. You can not fly a plane without the support of your co-pilot; in the same way, you cannot raise a child healthily without the support of the co-parent. There is no right path to raising a child, every child has unique needs, and so, the way you approach parenthood becomes innovative with every child. There is no set pattern or a book that you can follow to raise your child; rather, you have to figure out the child's needs in order to raise them right. This process can be expedited with the help of your co-pilot.

Post-divorce, co-parenting becomes extremely tough, especially when the parents do not get along. They are really good at fighting with each other, which makes the job tougher with time. Thus, I will be sharing some tips with you which will help make co-parenting much easier, as long as you follow them!

First and foremost, you should never involve your kids in your fights! This can be easily achieved by taking the co-parenting role as a new relationship. One that focuses on your kids and not on each other. Post-divorce, your relationship could be over, but your family is not. So, shape your new relationship by putting your kids' interests as the highest priority.

In addition to the previous point, you should always treat the other parent with respect. This will go a long way toward easing your relationship with your former partner in case you are divorced. If you are not divorced, then this point becomes more important for you as respecting your partner will result in a healthier environment in your household and will build on your children's wellbeing. This will also serve as a good model for your children. Our children imitate our behaviors and actions more than we are willing to admit. Disrespect toward the other parent will be played out by the child, or they will develop a certain image of that parent, not taking them too seriously. It is crucial for a child's healthy development to have respect for authority figures, including both parents. This will also allow them to have positive relationships with other authoritative figures as they progress in life, for example, their teachers, police officers, supervisors and government personnel.

You should also give the other parent enough space to think for the betterment of their children. It is good to observe appropriate boundaries when it comes to your kids. It becomes difficult to tell yourself that what the kids are doing with the other parent is 'none of my business.' Even though it should be like that in most cases where an activity with the other parent does not harm them physically or psychologically. You should give your partner and your kids that much space with each other; this requires trusting them as well. Recognize that it is okay, maybe even good, for children to learn different ways of doing things; they should be exposed to multiple perspectives. It is certain that neither the other parent nor your child will do everything your way. In fact, it is healthy for your child to be able to see a picture from different angles.

As discussed before, communicating with the other parent is vital in running a smooth team. There are so many things going on with your kids, and it is important to share all of that with the other parent so that they are more aware when dealing with them. You do not have to do this for the betterment of the parent, but do it for the child as the parent will be more helpful when they know things about their children. Thus, sharing information is also important. Especially when the children are young, the other parent needs to know the basics of parenting when some of the responsibilities are being transferred to them. It is good to be in a regular habit of sharing information with each other when co-parenting.

Also, if you demonstrate positive conflict resolution without involving the children in your fights, your house could be a recipe for success. You should not even try to hide things from your children. That's because most of them already know about what is going on. So, instead of keeping them as the flies on the wall, as discussed in the previous chapters, you should try to engage them in drafting a resolution. Just involving them in the process allows them to feel much more valuable. Using your conflicts as an opportunity to teach your kids how to resolve issues would be a responsible choice. You need to teach them to cool down before making an impulsive decision. "Do not step into the ring without taking the time to cool off," wise words by a friend of mine, is what I think should be taught to the children when dealing with conflicts.

Additionally, you should share with your co-parent what you need from him or her to do a good job while parenting. Suppose your kid has been caught lying in school? It is vital to share that information as the trait could be observed by the other parent without them knowing it. By sharing the information, you will allow the other parent to be more conscious of what they say and do. Moreover, they can take steps that can help curb the behavior displayed by your child. If they are not aware of the child's problem, they might add nothing of value or may even influence the child negatively. Everyone has different requirements for support. You should be clear with the other parent about your requirements and take time to inquire about theirs. Guesswork has never been much helpful in parenting, and so, you should help avoid guessing for yourself and your co-parent.

Furthermore, it is important to share your parenting tasks, do not allow all of the tasks to fall on one parent's shoulders. Things that are out of balance do not usually work. A lot of people compare a family to a car, meaning that a car cannot work without the support of all four tires. In the same way, a family cannot work without the support of all the members. If the car's weight is more on one side, do you expect the car to function normally in the long run? No, you have to spread the weight equally, just like with the tasks of parenthood. Try to share parenting chores as equally as possible. Do not hoard all the tasks, thinking that it might make you a better parent. Do not expect the other parent to do all the communication or all of the disciplining. Everything must work in balance to ensure a peaceful household.

As parents, you should always strive for consistency in disciplining, feeding and caring for your child. This makes transitions from one household to another easier, in the case of divorced parents. This also allows the minimization of the outbursts displayed by children after visits with the other parent. Respect each other's parenting approaches and recognize that while consistency is optimal, differences are acceptable too. Children are good at distinguishing that something which may be allowed at their father's house may not be tolerable at the mother's house. This is not because one parent is wrong and the other is right, it is because the two parents are different, and children do realize that.

Help your children appreciate the other parent with appropriate gifts and cards. Take the time out to help them plan or even make holiday and birthday gifts for the other parent. As discussed before, children are good at imitating what their parents do rather than what they say. Thus, do the things that you would want your kids to do for you, and be the right role model for them!

The last and one of the most important rules of co-parenting is to respect your in-laws just as much as your partner. Do not punish them by keeping them away from your kids after a divorce or breakup. You will only be hurting your kids by cutting off ties with them. I have heard kids complain about not being able to meet their cousins due to the disputes of the parents. It saddens me so much because the healthy relationships in a child's life are awfully significant in their development. When you impose such restrictions, you hinder their ability to maintain those relationships, which results in the children having commitment issues.

All of the tips that I have given you will help you, your partner and your kids. Remember, parenting is a two-way street; the efforts you make for the other parent will result in the other parent making efforts for you. You may not need the help right now, but someday you might. You should never let your ego stand in the way of the betterment of your child.

I have talked to many fathers who are unable to maintain a healthy relationship with their children due to the angst they feel about their exes. I have helped a lot of them understand that the only thing important in the whole situation is their children. One of the stories that I share in my classes is called, "When the student is ready, the teacher will appear."

Glen Warren Senior would always tell me that, "Most of us, if not all of us, hear what we are ready to hear. If we are not ready to hear it, no matter how sound the advice is, we won't hear it."

According to an old saying, "When the student is ready, the teacher will appear." There are several ways to interpret this statement. It could mean that when one is ready to learn, he or she will learn. Another interpretation might be that the desire to learn begets the experience to learn. Perhaps, it also means that when a person sees something clearly for the first time, even though it has always been there, maybe that person is finally ready to learn.

A teacher could be a person or a metaphor for a learning experience. Either way, it could be that the teacher is always ready to teach, but the student is not always ready to learn. The answers the student needs could have been out there all the while, but the student was not ready for them or was not aware that those answers were needed. Most of us, if not all of us, hear only what we are ready to hear. If we are not ready to hear it, no matter how sound the advice is, we won't hear it. Let's see how this saying relates to our subject when love is not enough.

This story is about a father; let's call him Billy, who was ready to learn. He was court-ordered to attend Fathers Forever, but unlike most of the men who were ordered by the court to attend, he was happy to come. His other choice was to go to jail. A few months prior to this court date, Billy had already spent three days in jail for non-payment of child support, and this time, he was facing 30 days. After he attended four parenting group sessions, we had our first individual parenting class. He said, "What you are telling us, I have heard many times, but I guess I wasn't ready to hear it." I asked him what had changed for him, and he said, "I guess now I am ready to change my life."

He began to share his life story with me, the good and the bad —mostly bad — about how he had not been taking care of his six children. He then said, "Mr. G, I made a lot of mistakes." I asked him to share some of them with me, and he told me of getting a DUI, quitting his job to avoid paying child support, assaulting a female, and breaking and entering.

I asked Billy if there was a difference between a choice and a mistake. He replied as if he never thought about that before, "I am not sure." I told him they are not one and the same, and I explained the difference to him, emphasizing that there is a distinct difference between them. He listened intently as I explained that a mistake is an error in judgment or a miscalculation.

"For example," I told him, "I stepped on your toe because I miscalculated where your foot was in relation to my step. That's a mistake. A choice, on the other hand, is when you decide to act on one of the many options available to you." I explained to Billy that getting a DUI was not a mistake because he had other options to choose from. I went on to tell him that sometimes people call bad choices mistakes, then justify those bad choices by saying, "Everybody makes mistakes" or "We all make mistakes." A person who makes such a statement is not taking responsibility for his or her choices, which can lead the person to continue making bad choices. However, once we call it what it is, a bad choice, we allow ourselves to take ownership of those choices. It is only then we can move forward to the path of making better choices.

As I restated the fact that getting a DUI was not a mistake; it was a choice because he had other options to choose from, he interrupted me and said, "Yeah, I could have called somebody to pick me up." In fact, he came up with several more options.

Then I said those four things you just listed as mistakes — getting a DUI, quitting your job to avoid paying child support, assaulting a female, and breaking and entering — were not mistakes but choices and bad choices. This time, he got it. The student was ready, and the teacher had appeared.

He began to tell me about his life as a father of six children by three different women and that he hadn't seen two of his children in three years. As for the other four, he sees them sporadically. His relationships with the three mothers are not good. He revealed that two of them call him a deadbeat dad, and the other mother, his former wife, has given up on him altogether: "She doesn't even come to court anymore."

She has remarried and moved on. He said, "Mr. G, I haven't been a good father to any of my children." He looked away, then down, trying to hide the tears that were filling his eyes.

I ended the session for that day.

It's been said, "Too much light too fast will blind you." I didn't want to blind him, but I did want him to see the error of his ways. That day's discussion was a beginning.

After a couple more group classes, we had another individual session, and the conversation went a little like this:

Billy: I really love my children, but I haven't been acting like it, have I?

Me: I guess sometimes love is not enough. (Billy looks at me, perplexed.)

Billy: Love is always enough.

Me: Love is a good thing, a very good thing, and love conquers all, but sometimes it's not enough. (Billy seems to be getting a little frustrated.) So, you love your children?

Billy: Yes, I do, with all of my heart.

Me: So why haven't you been taking care of them and supporting them? (Billy remains silent.)

Me: If a man or woman says they love their spouse and then

is unfaithful to them, do they really love their spouse?

Billy: Yeah, maybe.

Me: Perhaps he does, but their love is not enough to keep them faithful. (Billy looks away, another perplexed expression on his face.)

Me: Sometimes, Billy, love is not enough. (I end the session, this time on purpose by taking a phone call.)

At the next group class, Billy was kind of quiet, but he was engaging with everyone else and participating in the class discussion. As soon as we were alone, he asked me what I meant when I said "love was not enough," I corrected him: "I said sometimes love is not enough."

"So, what do you mean by that?" Billy asked. The student was ready; our session began.

Me: Who is the most important person in the car: the driver or the passengers?

Billy: The driver.

Me: Why?

Billy: The driver is the one in control of the car. The passengers don't control the car. They may give directions, but they are not in control.

I agreed with him, then step by step, I reminded him that the driver is responsible for the brakes, the steering, the speed, the signals and other lights, and everything that goes along with driving. Even when he is talking, he has to pay attention to all of the above and what is going on around the vehicle he is operating.

Billy looked really confused as if he was saying, "What has this got to do with the price of tea in China?"

Then I said, "Love is not enough when love is not the driver." I went on to tell him that love is sometimes put in the passenger seat or in the back seat, or even sometimes in the trunk as a piece of luggage. Love may be there in the car, but it is not in the driver's seat. Whatever is driving that car is not love. It could be anything from bitterness, anger, unforgiveness, selfishness, revenge to retaliation, but not love.

Then I asked him, "So, Billy, who has been driving the car as it relates to your children?" I went on to say, "Perhaps your love for them is in the passenger seat, the back seat or even in the trunk. Yes, your love is in the car, but your love needs to take back the wheel." Then I looked him in the eyes and said, "Man, there is no doubt in my mind that you love your children, but you have to decide who is doing the driving, your love for them or some of those other passengers I just named."

He sat there quietly.

My final statement to Billy that day was, "Let's go back to the spouse who was unfaithful. Perhaps their love wasn't driving the car; maybe their love was in the passenger seat, the back seat, or even in the trunk, and, yes, perhaps they, too, needed to let love take over the driving."

As we ended that session, Billy gave me a firm handshake and said, "Today, I'm taking back the wheel, and I'm getting some new passengers."

I looked away from him this time, trying to hide my tears. The student was ready. By the time Billy graduated from Fathers Forever, he had repaired his relationships with the mother of two of his children and was spending more time with all of his children. He found a steady job and paid his child support payments on time. He confided, "I am still working on the other mom."

At his graduation ceremony, Billy said, "Mr. Glen, I will NEVER let go of the wheel," to which I replied, "NEVER."

REVISION TIME!

Q. 1. Please fill out the blanks with the most appropriate answer from the brackets.

a) Parenting is more about the _____ rather than the biological relationship of the parents. (financial provisions, act of parenthood, disciplining methods, constant oversight)

b) _____ is the act of sharing the responsibilities of parenthood. (Joint Custody, Pooling, Child support, Co-parenting)

c) _____ with the other parent is vital in running a smooth team. (Communicating, Fighting, Budgeting, Playing)

d) It is easier to build strong _____ than to repair broken men. (institutions, fathers, jails, children, sentiments)

e) Do not step into the ring without taking the time to _____. (prepare, cool off, practice, cheat, eat)

Q. 2. Encircle 'True' or 'False' if you think the statements are right or wrong, respectively.

a) When the teacher is ready, the student will appear.

True   False

b) You can fly a plane without the support of your co-pilot, the same way you can raise a child healthily without the support of the co-parent.

True   False

c) Most of us, if not all of us, hear what we are ready to hear.

True   False

d) It's been said that too little light will blind you.

True   False

e) Parenting is a two-way street; the efforts you make for the other parent will result in the other parent making efforts for you.

True   False

Q. 3. Describe in a single line what you have learned by reading this chapter.

_____

Q. 4. Describe in a single line how you will be applying what you have learned in this chapter.

_____

Answer Key

Q. 1. a) Parenting is more about the <u>act of parenthood</u> rather than the biological relationship of the parents.

b) <u>Co-parenting</u> is the act of sharing the responsibilities of parenthood.

c) <u>Communicating</u> with the other parent is vital in running a smooth team.

d) It is easier to build strong <u>children</u> than to repair broken men.

e) Do not step into the ring without taking the time to <u>cool off</u>.

Q. 2. a) False.

b) False.

c) True.

d) False.

e) True.

Q. 3 & 4. If you do not have an answer, reread the chapter and try to take a lesson from it. There are no right or wrong answers for these.

Chapter 5

Anger Management

Anger can never be managed without the ways of
Forgiveness.

Gautama Buddha, the founder of Buddhism and a dedicated philosopher, mendicant, meditator, describes the devastation that can be caused by anger to oneself. He says, "Holding on to anger is like grasping a hot coal with the intent of throwing it at someone else; you are the one who gets burned." Buddha tries to explain that holding on to anger is more destructive to our own selves rather than the person who may have caused it. It is neither good for us nor for the receiver of our anger, as eventually, the other party will get hurt too, but we will be hurt the most in the process.

Nonetheless, it becomes very difficult for us to let go of it or to cope with it in a healthy way. Usually, we end up burning ourselves and others as we think projecting it will help us recover, which is not true in most cases. Then, how do we deal with this anger? Well, we will be discussing anger management and how it relates to co-parenting to help you deal with anger in a more constructive manner. As discussed before, anger and conflict are not only limited to the parents, even if they are the only ones involved. Rather, it transcends to the whole family or household, as they get affected in any conflict between the parents. Children always get affected when their parents are fighting, and different ways shall be constructed so as to avoid that. You want your children to cope with their anger, right? Well, as we learned in the previous chapters, we have to set the right examples in order for them to follow.

To deal with anger, we must understand what it is. Anger is a normal emotion with a wide range of intensity, from mild irritation and frustration to rage. It is a reaction to a perceived threat to ourselves, our loved ones, property, self-image, or some part of our identity. Anger is a warning bell that tells us that something is wrong.

Anger exists in the mind and is a direct result of our thoughts. It is not particularly an event that makes us angry, but our interpretation of the event and how we think and feel about it that can lead to anger. Certain things, such as mental and physical exercises, can be done to make the feelings of anger more controllable and manageable.

The process of anger can be broken down into three components, physical, mental and behavioral aspects. The physical reaction usually starts with a rush of adrenaline, increased heart rate, blood pressure and tightening muscles. As can be seen, anger can have disastrous effects on our own health, and so, managing it would be the most beneficial to ourselves, as well. Our children also learn how to deal with anger from us!

The cognitive experience of anger is, in simpler words, how we perceive and think about what is making us angry. For example, we might think that something that happened to us is wrong, unfair and undeserved. Again, this will only damage our own mental health as we only think about the wrongs that have been done to us. Instead of dealing with those issues, we just keep thinking about it, which makes the issue seem bigger than it actually is. Therefore, we find ourselves in a never-ending loop where we keep magnifying the issue and do nothing to resolve it.

The behavioral aspect is the way we express anger. There is a wide range of behaviors that signal it. We may look and sound angry, raise our voice, clam up, slam doors or storm away, all of which are signals of being angry. Now, you are not only hurting yourself but also those who are around you.

This will not be limited to the person you are angry at; it affects all of those in the vicinity of the conflict. For example, if you are angry at your wife, there are high chances that your kids will be affected as well. Maybe they are involved as the 'flies on the wall.' But they will be involved sooner or later, as both the parents will be affected, and in turn, will affect the way they deal with the children. Therefore, it becomes extremely important to control your anger, which could be done for yourself, your partner or your kids. Kids get extremely upset when they know their parents are fighting. They think of the worst outcomes, such as divorce, so it is crucial to control your anger as it affects your child's mental health too. Furthermore, anger can lead to things like unforgiveness, bitterness and resentment, which we will delve into in the next chapter.

Many people think that anger management classes are effective at dealing with anger, but those classes focus only on the behavioral aspect. Our focus is going to be much more holistic, capturing all the elements related to anger. If we think about it, it is pretty much like the rest of the emotions that are God-given such as happiness, sadness, embarrassment and so on. Remember, co-parenting can never be successful in an angry environment, and we have already established its importance in the previous chapter.

We must note that anger always leads to an overreaction. This happened with me and my significant other, Helen. Something caused us both to get angry. I was able to somewhat control my emotions, but she failed to do so. This resulted in her blasting off an email in anger. Thus, we had two problems on our hands now; one was the initial situation which led to anger, and then the overreaction, which led to further problems. Now, as I discussed before, if you do not resolve your anger in a constructive manner, then you will be stuck in a loop. In our case, we got angry, and our reactions only built on that anger. If she had controlled her anger like I did, we would not have two problems on our hands. Thus, controlling and managing your anger is crucial in running a household.

You can see a lot of people having anger issues on the road, which is termed as road rage. People get mad when somebody pulls up in front of them, even though they did not hit you or anything. It is the underlying anger that is feeding into your reaction. What happens next? You try to chase them down, curse at them or blow your horn at them. That is you overreacting to the situation, which might have just created another problem for you. For example, we hear stories of road rage, which leads to people getting in serious fights. Getting into a fight has its own consequences, and therefore, you have another problem at your disposal. Now, it should become evident that controlling your anger is beneficial for you and those around you. You must also control your reaction to the situation to avoid further problems for yourself and others. The overreaction could be physical, mental or behavioral, as discussed before.

I have been teaching some anger management classes as well, and there I met a lady who had severe anger issues. She would throw things at her husband in anger.-When I asked her why she behaved like that, her response was that something snaps inside her brain, and she ends up getting mad without the ability to control it. I figured she was having issues dealing with the mental and behavioral aspects. So, I asked her what she did for a living, and she told me that she was a customer service representative. That did not make much sense to me, and I asked her how she deals with angry clients without getting frustrated at work? Her reply to that was that she would end up getting fired if she reacted in such a way. I explained to her that as we think that our workplace behavior has major consequences like getting fired, we are able to control our anger. However, we assume that in our personal lives, there are no consequences.-But there definitely are! This anger can lead to separation, divorce or damage to children's wellbeing. Another thing that she helped me realize was that we are all able to control our anger. We are just unaware of the consequences, and therefore, act upon it rashly. But hopefully, you have understood the consequences of anger by now.

Thus, I will be explaining some effective ways of dealing with anger so that we can minimize the damage caused by its aftermath. One of the easiest and most effective methods is to think before you speak. In the heat of the moment, it is easy to say something that you will regret later. Take a few minutes to collect your thoughts before saying anything. Also, allow the others who are involved in the situation to do the same as well. When an event has occurred which causes anger, delay the response to it by taking a 'timeout.' Once you are calm, you will be able to project your anger in a healthier way. You will be thinking clearly after giving yourself some time. You will still express your frustrations in an assertive manner, but it will be less confrontational. In such scenarios, try to state your concerns clearly and directly, without hurting others or trying to dominate them. The reason why you want to let the anger out is because unexpressed anger builds on your problems, leading to pathological expressions of anger, such as passive-aggressive behavior, i.e., getting back at people indirectly without telling them why, rather than confronting them head-on.

Angry people are always putting others down, and so, it is way better to focus on the solutions rather than the problems. You should be more proactive about the situation rather than being reactive, i.e., shift your focus from being defensive to an offensive approach to finding a solution. Remind yourself that anger will not fix anything, it will only make matters worse.

Furthermore, try not to hold on to a grudge. Forgiveness is a very powerful tool, which will be the main topic in the next chapter. If you allow anger and other negative feelings to crowd out positive feelings, you might find yourself swallowed up in bitterness or a sense of injustice. However, if you forgive someone who angered you, both of you might end up learning from the situation. It is unrealistic to expect anyone to behave exactly as you would want them to, at all times. So the least you can do is understand their point of view and clear up any misunderstandings.

You should also practice relaxation skills and try to get some exercise to blow off that steam. When your temper flares, put those relaxation skills at work. You can practice deep-breathing exercises; imagine a relaxing scene, or even repeat a calming word or phrase such as 'take it easy' or 'all is well.' Some people find meditating and yoga as extremely effective methods for calming their anger. Religious and spiritual activities, such as going to church, can also help some people calm themselves. Moreover, physical activity can help reduce stress caused by anger. If you feel that your anger is escalating, you should go for a brisk walk, run, or any such physical activity, which, if enjoyable, will be more beneficial.

You should also know when to seek help. Learning to control anger is a challenge for everyone. You should consider seeking help if your anger seems out of control and leads you to do things you regret or hurt those around you.

Everyone experiences anger and it can be healthy at times. It can motivate us to stand up for ourselves and correct injustice. When we manage anger well, it prompts us to make positive changes in our lives and situations.

Mismanaged anger, on the other hand, is counterproductive and can be unhealthy. When anger becomes too intense, out of control, misdirected and overly aggressive, it can lead to poor decision making and problem-solving. Mismanaged anger creates problems in your relationships, at work and can even affect your health. I will be sharing some short stories which will further clarify how unhealthy mismanaged anger is. I refer to these stories as "Unintended consequences."

The term unintended consequences describes a set of results that were not intended as an outcome. It also means the effect, result, or outcome of something that occurred earlier. For example, an accident is the consequence of reckless driving. Parents are sometimes the cause of the emotional accidents our children are involved in because of emotional reckless driving. We don't intend for the accidents to happen — they are unintended, but they happen, and our kids end up suffering from them the most.

Let's look at some examples of emotional reckless driving.

Emotional Reckless Driving Incident # 1 (Couple)

A mother denies her children the right to meet their father because the father has moved in with his new girlfriend and started another family on the other side of town. The father is required to pay child support and is granted visitation rights, but after many attempts to see his children with no success, he just gives up and focuses on paying his child support. He doesn't see his three children at all. He declares, "I will just see them when they get to be 18." However, one day, he gets a call from the mother: one of his sons has joined a gang and is now being charged with breaking and entering and grand theft auto. When asked why he joined the gang, the son replies, "The gang protects me since my mother won't let me see my Daddy, and my Daddy seems to have forgotten about us. He doesn't even call or come visit us."

I am not sure what the mother's motive was for denying the father the opportunity to see his children, and I am not sure why the father didn't fight for his right to see his children, but this tragic situation is the outcome of their decision, an unintended consequence: the son now has a criminal record that could affect him for the rest of his life. He had just turned 18.

Emotional Reckless Driving Incident # 2 (Father)

The father refused to pay child support, moving from job to job, address to address, to avoid paying child support, and declaring he would rather go to jail than pay child support for his 16-year-old son because the mother was using the money to get her hair done. His son was approached by a drug dealer, and he started selling drugs. When asked by his probation officer why he started selling drugs, he stated that he had to help his mother pay their bills. They had been on the verge of getting evicted several times, and he didn't want them to be homeless. The son is now incarcerated for possession, trafficking, and selling cocaine. I am sure the father didn't mean for that unintended consequence to happen, but it did.

Emotional Reckless Driving Incident # 3 (Mother)

The parents of a 15-year-old girl separated, and later they got a divorce. She was very close to her father and was allowed to spend the weekends with him until the father remarried. Then the mother stopped allowing the girl to see her father. After a few months, the mother moved to another city, changed her phone number, and would not allow her daughter to contact him. The daughter became depressed to the point that her friends were very concerned. One day, the daughter didn't come to school, and the mother was contacted by a school administrator because her friends had told their teacher about their concerns.

The mother rushed home and found her daughter unresponsive in her bed, with an empty bottle of her prescription medication lying beside her. She had taken an overdose, but fortunately, her mother had found her in time. She was rushed to the hospital and suffered no permanent damage.

A few days later, the girl was asked by her counselor why she had wanted to end her life. The girl stated, "My mother won't let me see my dad. She won't even let me talk to him, and I don't want to live without my dad." I am sure that was not the result the mother wanted; however, what happened with her daughter was an unintended consequence that almost cost her daughter's life.

Emotional Reckless Driving Incident # 4 (Father)

This well-groomed, educated, very articulate father was struggling with a lot of negative emotions when I first met him. He was 32 years old and had a seven-year-old son. He was recently divorced from his child's mother after eight years of marriage. He was very angry, bitter, and hurt. He was hurt about the break-up: his world had turned upside down. After being separated for a couple of months, they decided to go to counseling. They moved back in together, hoping to work things out. He stated their reconciliation didn't last too long, and soon they separated again. She told him she just wasn't in love with him anymore.

His wife met with a lawyer, and the father was served with divorce papers. Again, his world was turned upside down. He was a broken man as he sat, crying in my office. He said,

"I am still in love with my wife and I haven't seen my son in over a year. I pay my child support, but I can't seem to forgive her for all the pain she has caused me. But now my son is in trouble. He has been suspended for the rest of the year because he brought a knife to school and threatened another student and a teacher. My ex-wife says it is my fault. My son has been calling me, but I don't answer his calls sometimes. I say I will call him back, but I don't. My ex-wife says he is angry all the time. She put him in counseling but that hasn't helped."

The father was angry, and so was his son. Both were victims of the unintended consequences of anger and bitterness. I am sure this father didn't set out for this to happen, but nevertheless, it did.

Emotional Reckless Driving Incident # 5 (Mother)

When a witness is due to speak officially in court, he or she takes an oath before he or she testifies or gives evidence. The witness usually swears the oath while his or her hand is on a Bible or some other sacred item. The idea is that once the witness has taken this oath, he or she can be charged with perjury if found to be lying. But why is the phrase so long? And why does it sound redundant? There are three parts, and each means something different. The full oath is "I swear that the evidence that I shall give shall be the truth, the whole truth and nothing but the truth, so help me God. Affirmation: I solemnly affirm that the evidence that I shall give, shall be the truth, the whole truth and nothing but the truth." Truth is regarded as the correct information as far as the person is aware. The whole truth means that nothing must be omitted, and the person can't leave out any details. Nothing but the truth means no speculation can be made, and there can be no additions to the truth.

Sitting in family court one day, as I watched a case unfold, I had a better understanding and appreciation of how this oath works. Let's call this couple Ben and Cathy. This couple had been married for 18 years, and they had three children, all under the age of 16. Cathy reported that they had been having marital problems for the last three years, and she wanted a divorce. Ben had been unfaithful, and when he refused to move out, Cathy contacted a lawyer, who started the divorce proceedings that would give her an edge over her soon to be ex-husband. The strategy was to open a domestic violence case against Ben. She did so by starting an argument during which she tried to provoke him to hit her. Even though that strategy failed, she called the police anyway and accused him of grabbing and pushing her down. When the police arrived, she showed them a bruise on her arm, though Ben had not inflicted it, of course. Ben was taken to jail and charged with domestic violence. As a result, Ben lost his job because he had missed too many days, and a restraining order was issued against him by the court.

At the hearing, Cathy did not tell the truth, the whole truth, and nothing but the truth. Cathy now had the edge, and they were later divorced. Ben couldn't find steady work because of the domestic violence charge; therefore, he couldn't pay his child support. Cathy couldn't afford the house note alone, so the house went into foreclosure and she had to move into a temporary shelter with their three children. One by one, the children began to have issues in school, including poor grades and poor attendance. The oldest son started using drugs. In counseling, the oldest son declared, "My parents have ruined my life. I liked my friends, my school, and my neighborhood, but now we are living in a shelter. I don't care anymore about anything. All I want to do is get high."

I am sure that is not the outcome Ben and Cathy had in mind. Especially Cathy, who expected her lies to produce a different result.

These are just a few stories. I suppose I could write a book on this segment alone. It is so sad that a lot of our children's lives are so affected by our decisions, which I call the emotional reckless driving of some parents, which causes very negative unintended consequences.

Please, let's stop breaking our children.

95

REVISION TIME!

Q. 1. Please fill out the blanks with the most appropriate answer from the brackets.

a) Holding on to anger is like grasping a hot coal with the intent of throwing it at someone else; you are the one who gets _____. (revenge, burned, happy, the reward)

b) Anger and conflict are not only limited to the parents if they are the ones involved; rather, it transcends to _____. (the whole family, their friends, life, coparenting)

c) Anger exists in the mind and is a direct result of your _____. (actions, co-parenting, thoughts, behaviors)

d) _____ can never be successful in an angry environment. (Fighting, Budgeting, Co-parenting, Sports)

e) Angry people are always putting _____ down. (emotions, their foot, children, themselves, others)

Q. 2. Encircle 'True' or 'False' if you think the statements are right or wrong, respectively.

a) Mismanaged anger creates problems in your relationships.

True   False

b) Everyone experiences anger, and it can be healthy.

True   False

c) Once you are calm, you will not be able to project your anger in a healthier way.

True   False

d) The term unintended consequences describes a set of results that were intended as an outcome.

True   False

e) One of the easiest and most effective methods to control anger is to speak before you think.

True   False

Q. 3. Describe in a single line what you have learned by reading this chapter.

_____

Q. 4. Describe in a single line how you will be applying what you have learned in this chapter.

_____

Answer Key

Q. 1. a) Holding on to anger is like grasping a hot coal with the intent of throwing it at someone else; you are the one who gets <u>burned</u>.

b) Anger and conflict are not only limited to the parents if they are the ones involved; rather, it transcends to <u>the whole family</u>.

c) Anger exists in the mind and is a direct result of your <u>thoughts</u>.

d) <u>Co-parenting</u> can never be successful in an angry environment.

e) Angry people are always putting <u>others</u> down.

Q. 2. a) True.

b) True.

c) False.

d) False.

e) False.

Q. 3 & 4. If you do not have an answer, reread the chapter and try to take a lesson from it. There are no right or wrong answers for these.

Chapter 6

Forgiveness

Forgiveness is essential on the journey of peace and happiness.

Nelson Mandela, the former and the first black President of South Africa, a remarkable leader, who dismantled apartheid and was a strong activist for equality, said, "Resentment is like drinking poison and then hoping it will kill your enemies." He tries to explain here that there is no point in not forgiving as it only builds on your frustration and stress. When you do not forgive, you keep the hate within yourself, which destroys you rather than the other person. Thus, forgiveness is not only beneficial to the other party; rather, it is more beneficial to oneself as it brings peace of mind and cleanliness of the heart.

A lot of people believe that marriages thrive on love, trust, companionship, and sacrifice. However, I believe that any successful marriage requires both spouses to be able to forgive each other as mistakes are made by everyone and can be made quite often. If you let your ego stand in the way of forgiveness, it will become really difficult for you to be in a marriage and maintain a family successfully.

In order to understand forgiveness, we must define it first. Forgiveness is the willingness to give up your resentment toward someone who has wronged you, regardless of how serious or painful that wrong might have been. That means you renounce any desire to get even. As I have said before, co-parenting requires you to be understanding of your partner rather than making it a competition. You have to let go of your ego for your kids, yourself, and your partner. More importantly, forgiveness should be more than just saying the words "I forgive you." It must come from your heart, i.e., you must actually mean it instead of just saying it. If you do not forgive from the heart, then the resentment and frustration will never allow for healthy companionship or a healthy household.

As discussed, unforgiveness is poisonous for your own soul. It is a deliberate mindset to resent the wrong and wrongdoer. It is a means of seeking revenge that can turn into a nasty battle between both the partners, which transcends to the children as well. Unforgiveness is associated with bitterness, wrath, anger, slander and malice, all the things that we wanted to get rid of, as discussed in the previous chapter; anger management. Your anger can never be managed if you do not learn the art of forgiveness, and we have already established the importance of controlling your anger. Thus, anger management and forgiveness work together; without one, the other would fail to flourish.

Unforgiveness chooses painful attitudes over tenderness, gentleness, and a forgiving mindset. Many people, these days, become physically ill because they choose to keep those negative emotions instead of the positive ones. They live, day by day, year by year, with the cancer of an unforgiving heart. The reason why I call it cancer is because it slowly eats away your heart and soul, leaving them immensely damaged. Now, I know forgiving is extremely difficult in the beginning, but once you start practicing it, you will understand how beneficial it is for all the parties involved. You will never go back to stressing or fighting over small matters. The truth is that people choose to be unforgiving, which, for me, is a deliberate decision of self-inflicted pain.

There are three major elements in forgiving; to give up resentment about the wrong and wrongdoer while also giving up plans for retaliation. If you can successfully incorporate these three key elements when you forgive someone, that means you have done it truly from the heart. Otherwise, there will not be any point in forgiving as, even if one element fails, it will be cancerous for you and those around you.

After incorporating the three elements, the question that arises is how do you know that you have truly forgiven someone? Well, there are two indications that show you just that. The first is that your feelings toward the other person will have changed. You will have more positive emotions toward them rather than negative emotions. You will be happy to see them, and your painful memories of them won't be triggered. Whenever you see them, you will be able to feel that the resentment is gone, given that you have truly forgiven. The second indication is linked to the first, i.e., you will know your forgiveness is genuine when you feel concerned about the other person rather than feeling hateful or indifferent toward them. You will start caring about your partner's welfare, and you will want the best for them instead of planning how to get back at them. Once you feel that the two have been accomplished, you will feel much more at ease, and your heart will become much lighter than when you were carrying hate toward them.

Paul Boese, a film actor, says, "Forgiveness does not change the past, but it does enlarge the future." What he means by this is that forgiveness will not make you forget what happened or remove that memory of your past; rather, it stops that negativity from spreading in your life and those around you. It actually allows a better future for both parties involved and can result in a better relationship than before. The reason being that it shows the other person that you are willing to accept them for their mistakes and not just their best form. It shows them that you care, and so, it allows for the two of you to respect each other even more, bringing you closer and happier with each other.

Forgiveness entails two other components as well, apologies and promises. Both are extremely hard to do, but again, once you start practicing it and have a hold on it, you will realize how important these tools are in anger management and forgiveness. Moreover, it allows a healthy relationship to be formed between the parents and the children.

An apology is a genuine expression of regret or remorse for having said or done something that offended someone. An apology can go a long way which can manifest in many ways, but Toba Beta, an author, describes the importance of apologies beautifully, "In this life, when you deny someone an apology, you will remember it at the time you beg forgiveness." Toba explains that throughout your life, at different moments, you can be on both the giving or receiving end. So it is important to be able to forgive because you will need forgiveness someday as well. As I have said, we all make mistakes, some more often than others, but we all do so, when you get angry at someone else's mistake, think about a time when you did the same. You probably were thinking that it is not as bad as the other person is thinking or maybe that the other person does not love you enough to overlook your shortcomings. Well, the way you expect to be forgiven, so does your partner, and when you shower them with your anger, you just push them far away. Thus, whenever you are angry, think about how vulnerable you felt when you made a mistake and try to put yourself in the other person's shoes. Act the way you would want to be treated when you made a mistake.

A promise, on the other hand, is an agreement to do something for someone. An apology is as binding as a promise; both of them result in an agreement. In the case of an apology, it is an agreement to not do something again on behalf of the perpetrator and an agreement on behalf of the offended to forgive the trespass. There is another thing to keep in mind when apologizing to someone, as Kimberly Johnson, an American poet, says, "Never ruin an apology with an excuse." The whole point of apologizing is to show that you have accepted your fault and you want to make up for your wrongdoing. By offering an excuse alongside the apology, you are not fully accepting your fault; instead, you are blaming something else for your mistake. Thus, the other person will feel that you really are not apologizing; rather, you are just making excuses for yourself. Therefore, in order to wholly accept your mistake and offer a wholehearted apology, never give excuses, even if you have some.

In arguments, both the parties want to end with their statement, i.e., they want to make sure that they say the closing statement in an argument, which is a way of not accepting defeat. Yet, if you play smartly, you can have the last word along with being the bigger person. All you have to do is end the argument with an apology. Lynn Johnston, a Canadian cartoonist, and author, says, "An apology is the superglue of life, it can repair just about anything." I truly believe in that saying because no matter what the extent of your mistake is, if you can apologize wholeheartedly and try to make it up to the other person as badly as you made a mistake, you can repair any broken relationship. No one wants to hate someone forever; words can do a lot to bring that bond back that you once, may have had.

"When you realize that you have made a mistake, make amends immediately. It is easier to eat crow while it is still warm," as said by Dan Heist, shows the importance of apologizing as soon as you have realized your fault. Even if you haven't realized it, if you think you might be at fault, apologize; it will not make you less of a person. Moreover, if you apologize after some time has passed, it will make the job much harder because the resentment has grown over time for both parties. Thus, try to apologize straight away so that the other person does not start thinking deeply about what you might have done or said to them. Instead, apologize quickly so that they can think about your apology instead of focusing just on your fault.

A lot of times, you will find yourself apologizing, but you will not mean it. That kind of apology is useless because you will repeat the same mistake again and again. You might keep apologizing for it, but it will mean nothing to your partner. You are just saying it instead of acting upon it. Thus, you should use the two tools of forgiveness; apologize and promise. Apologize for what you have done wrong and promise not to repeat the same thing again. If you can fulfill your promise, you will not have to apologize for the same thing again; plus, your partner will respect you more for keeping your promise.

Even though anger management and forgiveness are aspects that cannot be taken lightly or ignored, I suggest refraining from getting worked up in the first place. This way, you won't fall into a situation where you might have to ask for forgiveness. Moreover, if you forgive someone, do it nicely instead of rubbing it in their face. Always remember to keep your words soft so that they do not come back to haunt you. As they say, what goes around comes around, so try to avoid bitterness and anger in the first place so that you do not have to face it someday from someone else. Try to avoid fights, bad language, blaming, shouting, and so on. Also, teach all this to your children as well so that they grow up to be nice people. As we have discussed, the best way to teach your children is by action. You are your child's role model and so, imagine how you want your child to be when they grow up because that is who you should strive to be now.

Teach your children the value of forgiveness, promises, and apologies so that they can grow up to be respected individuals. If your children do not forgive you for your mistakes, how would that make you feel? Thus, if you can not be nice to your partner for their sake, do it for yourself and for your children. It will allow them to respect both the parents much more when they see that their egos are smaller than the value they have for their family, instead of the other way around. In the latter case, your children will be inclined to be disrespectful toward you when they grow up.

I was in a relationship around 10 – 15 years ago, and everything was going smoothly, but the woman had an unforgiving heart. I decided that I could not be in a relationship with someone who was so unforgiving because you can not be intimate in a relationship if unforgiveness triumphs as that causes bitterness. Thus, forgiveness is a key element in any relationship.

There was a woman who got bit by a raccoon and went to the doctor to get herself checked. The doctor informed her that she had rabies, and she pulled out a piece of paper and started writing. The doctor asked her what she was writing, assuming that it is probably a diary or something of that nature. The lady was actually making a list of all the people she intended to bite. That shows how damaging unforgiveness and anger really are. Please, do not be like that lady. Even if she would have bitten all the people on her list, she would never be at peace because she still would not have forgiven them and might think that the revenge is probably not as bad as what they did to her. Thus, putting oneself in a vicious cycle of bitterness and self-destruction is not a good choice.

Suicides among men have risen over the last few years.

It used to be 7 out of 10 men committing suicide. Now, it has increased to 8 out of 10 men. One of the major reasons for this increase is that men bury their pain deep inside themselves. We do not know how to release that pain in a healthy manner. We walk around with an unforgiving heart, and nobody can tell any difference until one day when we explode by either killing ourselves or lashing out at someone. We may not even know why because the anger manifests inside and eventually acts on its own.

Men instill the same ideology of hiding their pain in their kids. For example, whenever a child falls down and is bleeding or has a bruise, what do we tell them? We tell them that nothing has happened and that everything is alright. The kid can see the blood coming out, but the parents are teaching him/her to hide the pain. Thus, the child grows up learning to hide the pain. We do this very often as parents.-We tell our children not to cry over things; that is also a way of telling them to hide their pain. Now, when that kid has a girlfriend, she will want him to show his emotions and be sensitive. However, the kid has always been taught the opposite, and so, as an adult, he has to face this conflict. Then it becomes really hard for anyone to tell that he is in pain because he gets so good at hiding it.

Many marriages fail because of this dilemma. Men start giving up on their marriages without expressing their concerns. Even though the frustration is being built for a long time, it seems like one day, they just get up and leave. They suddenly announce that they are done with the marriage. The wives never know that something is wrong, and they think that the man just gave up instantaneously. Thus, the men leave their marriage, their family, but the truth is that they had already quit a long time ago.

God made both man and woman and gave them the ability to cry for a reason. He wants us to express ourselves. He wants us to cry, but we stop ourselves from doing so, which is very unhealthy. We need to cry because we need a place to let our pain out. You might wonder what all this has to do with parenting, but expressing yourself is a very important element in anger management and forgiveness. Expressing anger in the right way is what we are talking about. It is better to cry rather than fighting, shouting or slandering.

We try to co-parent with an unforgiving heart, but that just does not work! If you are not willing to put anger aside, you will never move on for the rest of your life. You will always be stuck in that bitterness and resentment. Your marriage will be more of a battle than a relationship. However, you have the choice to change that. Forgiveness is for yourself and your kids. The kids should always be your number one priority.

"It's no pleasure to watch indifferent people argue. It is even worse when they are trying to co-parent." I have a story related to that philosophy; I call it "Unrealistic Expectations." The story is based on the blinders that are put on a horse to keep the horse focused on what is ahead.

The purpose of blinders is to limit what can be seen. We put blinders — a pair of leather flaps attached to a bridle — on horses to prevent them from seeing what they have the ability to see. The blinders prevent side vision, thus allowing them only to see straight ahead to what is in front of them.

Let's see how this works with people who have on a different type of blinders: the blinders of indifference.

The definition of indifference is a lack of feeling, interest, or concern for another; an emotional detachment; the absence of the capacity to feel for the other person. Some synonyms of indifference are apathy, insensibility, nonchalance, and cold-heartedness. It's no pleasure to watch indifferent people argue, and it is even worse when they are trying to co-parent.

Sitting in family court one day, I witnessed a former couple who had on the blinders of indifference. They had been in and out of court many times because they just couldn't agree on much of anything: visitation, who would provide medical insurance, or even which daycare center to use. They were both looking straight ahead, and both had the desire to one-up each other. The blinders of indifference would not allow them to see what they had the ability to see: the other parent's current struggle. Neither one could see the dysfunction they were showing their children, nor could either see the unreasonable requests they were asking of the court system. They seemed to expect the system to fix their indifference, their apathy, their insensibility, their nonchalant attitudes, and the cold-hearted way they were dealing with each other.

That painful 45-minute court session ended with another court date being set and with no clear resolution in sight. It seemed that they both wanted the court system to fix a problem that wasn't designed to fix. The court system could not adjust their attitudes, heal their past wounds, or correct their attitudes of indifference. I watched the countenances of the judge and the other court officials. It appeared that even they were frustrated and, at times, perplexed as to what the couple wanted from each other. Frankly, so was I. Each couple (person) has to find a way to take off the blinders of indifference if they are going to be effective co-parents. The legal system was not designed to help them make the necessary changes. The court system monitors the guidelines of visitation and custody; however, the parents have to monitor their behavior to each other on their own.

Love is a powerful force: love is freedom, love gives, and love forgives. If indifference is the opposite of love, then it must also be a powerful force. But indifference takes love away; it holds grudges, and it puts limitations on our ability to see what we have the ability to see. Co-parenting in itself has many challenges, but when both parents are wearing the blinders of indifference, they are failing at effective co-parenting.

If it is true that the opposite of love is not hate but indifference, then parents need to stay clear of indifference. Most people don't hate their former spouses, but they are often indifferent toward them. There are times the love for their children is not enough to keep former couples from fighting and hurting one another as they walk down the path of indifference.

So, parents, for your children's sake, you don't have to wear the blinders of indifference. Your love for them should be more than enough to take off the blinders in order to see what you each have the ability to see: the welfare of the children is the most important factor for you to consider. It's been said, "The best parent is both parents," and both need to be equally involved in the rearing of their children. Indifference stops love from flowing. There is no doubt the couple in this story loved their three children, but the love couldn't flow as long as the parents kept those blinders on.

REVISION TIME!

Q. 1. Please fill out the blanks with the most appropriate answer from the brackets.

a) _____ is like drinking poison and then hoping it will kill your enemies. (Love, Marriage, Gossiping, Resentment)

b) _____ is the willingness to give up your resentment toward someone who has wronged you, regardless of how serious or painful that wrong might have been. (Forgiveness, Marriage, Commitment, Parenting)

c) There are three major elements in forgiving; to give up resentment about the wrong and wrongdoer, while also giving up plans for _____. (divorce, retaliation, your benefit, resentment)

d) _____ is a genuine expression of regret or remorse for having said or done something that offended someone. (Obsessive eating, Crying, Pity, An apology)

e) Suicides among men have _____ over the last few years. (declined, remained constant, risen, died, doubled)

Q. 2. Encircle 'True' or 'False' if you think the statements are right or wrong, respectively.

a) Love is a powerful force: love is freedom; love gives, and love forgives.

True   False

b) Despite the importance of anger management and forgiveness, you should strive to avoid both things altogether.

True   False

c) Forgiveness does not change the past, but it does enlarge the future.

True   False

d) Co-parenting in itself has many challenges, but when both parents are wearing the blinders of indifference, they are succeeding at effective co-parenting.

True   False

e) When you realize that you have made a mistake, make amends after some time has passed.

True   False

Q. 3. Describe in a single line what you have learned by reading this chapter.

_____

Q. 4. Describe in a single line how you will be applying what you have learned in this chapter.

_____

Answer Key

Q. 1. a) <u>Resentment</u> is like drinking poison and then hoping it will kill your enemies.

b) <u>Forgiveness</u> is the willingness to give up your resentment toward someone who has wronged you, regardless of how serious or painful that wrong might have been.

c) There are three major elements in forgiving; to give up resentment about the wrong and wrongdoer while also giving up plans for <u>retaliation</u>.

d) <u>An apology</u> is a genuine expression of regret or remorse for having said or done something that offended someone.

e) Suicides among men have <u>risen</u> over the last few years.

Q. 2. a) True.

b) True.

c) True.

d) False.

e) False.

Q. 3 & 4. If you do not have an answer, reread the chapter and try to take a lesson from it. There is no right or wrong answer for these.

Chapter 7

Openness

Children can be like flowers, they both need nurturing to blossom.

Mother Teresa, missionary and nun, who dedicated her life to serve the poor and needy, describes how openness is vital in building your values. She said, "The openness of our hearts and minds can be measured by how wide we draw the circle of what we call family." Teresa has explained that being selfless is correlated with having an open mind which would allow you to incorporate as much goodness as you can in your life.

Manifesting peace and harmony when you are co-parenting is the most important action you can take for the betterment of your child. When carrying out your responsibility as a parent, use your words and talk to your partner. Just imagine yourself as a toddler. If you had gotten hurt or were in a problem, you would tell an elder the issue, and they would try to resolve it for you. In the same way, it is essential to segment your frame of mind and not bottle it up. It's therapeutic to share your feelings which can only occur if you incorporate openness with sincerity in your conversations. Talking is a natural phenomenon that is healthy to do especially when you have a disagreement or are in crisis.

Talking builds a connection, and it's the first step toward an outcome that is feasible for you as you have taken action. If you share your concerns and open up, you hear yourself and pay attention to what is going in your head. When you are faltering, it is difficult to remain optimistic, and sometimes your thoughts go awry. In these times, it is crucial to maintain a positive outlook which occurs when you share and vent. Make sure that whoever you are talking to or seeking advice from is actively looking out for you. Your listener cannot be just anyone; it has to be someone you can trust and who you believe has your back. The one you choose should let you take the lead and listen to you without judgment.

As a father, it is necessary that you procure a positive mindset if you are discussing your children. In the back of your head have a clear strategy of thinking the best for them. The way you think affects your behavior and your course of action. Even if you feel like spilling your negative thoughts, do it but in return, make a list of positive statements that will outweigh the negative.

If you talk and share your thoughts, you will feel relief taking over you. Your emotions will be validated as your listener may offer you guidance and give you advice that you can apply practically. Expressing yourself is difficult for quite a few people, and I admire people who make an effort to be vocal and communicate.

For relationships to flourish, make it evident that you are available to talk it out. It is always a viable option to converse and exchange different ideas on the upbringing of your children. The decisions you will make for them instead of arguing and fighting, will, in return, create misunderstanding. You may not realize it at the moment, but sharing builds closeness and makes your bond stronger for the future. Sharing the results of your experiences in powerful connections and you will recognize that other individuals also have similar stories as you. Being true to yourself and others is beneficial to both parties, whether it's your children or your co-parenting partner.

On the other hand, honesty between you and your child is key if you want them to trust you. Honesty should be encouraged and applied at home. Having an open discussion and heart-to-heart about why honesty is necessary will invoke principles in your child and teach them the value of truth. In the real world, a child's ethics and values will be continuously tested when they grow up. The training needs to start at home. A child must be, directly and indirectly, reminded that holding your ground is a requirement of being honest. People try to manipulate you, complicate a situation, but a child should be told to be consistent when presenting their side of the story. A child should be taught to manifest awareness when interacting with others by telling them to take notice when they feel they are being misused. Let your child know that telling the truth may seem difficult, but it serves its purpose in the end as it always pulls through by differentiating right from wrong. As a parent, you may have lied yourself as a child and may garner empathy toward your child, but it is much better to rationalize and call out their misconduct. Discuss the consequences of dishonesty, make communication and encourage using words instead of vindicating passive-aggressive behavior.

For example, if your daughter has broken a vase, don't ask her, "Did you break the vase?" or blame her as it will lead her to believe that she has a way out. Instead, ask her to clean up the mess. There will be other days when she will have plenty of chances to speak truthfully. Children observe their elders and watch what kind of action we take in tough situations. Ask yourself, are you practicing honesty and incorporating integrity in your daily life?

Praise your child when they tell you the truth and applaud their honesty as positive affirmations lead to a child repeating similar behavior, which got them admiration.

In order to instill values in your child's life, changing your perception is essential. You may not be able to change what happened in your life, but you can change the way you look at what happened in your life. This will eventually lead you forward. Incorporating courage and confidence in our children as fathers is part of our responsibility to lead our families. If we're not confident in who we are and if we don't have the courage, we can't lead our children to do what they need to do. Let me tell you about a well-known guy named Stephen Covey. He wrote several books, and one of them was Seven Habits of Highly Effective People. I use its teachings in my daily life, and it has changed my view on life. It helped me transform my perception of various situations that weren't in my control.

For instance, if you think you are a victim, then you're always going to have a victim mentality. You're always going to play the role of a victim. If you think you are a conqueror and a person who could get things done, your perception has got to change that way, and your behavior is going to be the same.

If you don't change your perception, you will continuously do the wrong thing, which will lead to constantly getting bad results. This philosophy began to change my life many years ago, even before I started Fathers Forever. In fact, that's one of the reasons why I began because I had to change my perception about what I'm doing.

Let me tell you a story shared by Stephen Covey. He would travel to visit his mother every Sunday morning on a train, read his newspaper and enjoy his alone time. One particular Sunday, a father and three children got on the train, and about three stops into the trip after they get on, Stephen got frustrated because the father was zoned-out and not paying attention to his children, a little girl, and two little boys. Everybody looked around at each other and then looked at the father, but he was just sitting there as the children made a fuss. Stephen got quite disturbed with this, and he put his newspaper onto the chair, got up, went up to the father and tapped him on his shoulder, and said, "Sir, can you please help with your kids? These kids are all over the place." As soon as he said that the father snapped back to reality and apologized. He said, "Oh, I'm sorry. I really am sorry. Their mom just died, and we're on the way back home." Steve was taken aback. He sat down and, for the rest of the trip, played with the three children.

What happened to Stephen Covey? What made his behavior change? The answer is he had a paradigm shift which means he made a change in his underlying assumptions. This highlights the fact that when your perception changes, your behavior changes. When your behavior changes, it changes the paradigm shift. Now this father just lost his wife. The kids just lost their mom, and for the rest of the trip, Stephen Covey is taking care of those kids. We need a paradigm shift in how we think about fatherhood. We need a paradigm shift of how we think about ourselves sometimes because once you have that paradigm shift, your behavior is going to change.

Our perception about fatherhood and life sometimes needs to change, and we need to be challenged. Sometimes it's good to have people come up to you and speak volumes into your life that helps you to change your life. If you are living in the past, then your past is dictating your present. If you live in the future, then your future is dictating your present. Let me tell you a story to further refine my point.

I was driving home on the Beltline on a rainy, cold Thursday afternoon. I was sitting in my car. The traffic had slowed down, and all of a sudden, out of the blue, a lady slammed into the back of my car. The freshly brewed coffee that I had bought for myself spilled all over the place. My hand jammed into the steering wheel. I was in too much pain to call the ambulance. The rescue squad came and took me to the hospital. My back and wrist were injured. Doctors gave me medicine; therefore, I went home and went to sleep. I relaxed and rested for four days. The next day, I was supposed to go to my chiropractor appointment. As I was driving, I kept looking at my review mirror, and every time a car would approach me from the back, I felt afraid. I almost ran into the back of a person as I watched my review mirror. Then it dawned on me that I barely paid attention to the windshield.

Sometimes in life, we are looking in the review mirror. We're looking back at our past failures and our past experiences. We are looking in the review mirror instead of looking at the windshield of life. There's a reason why the review mirror is much smaller than the windshield. We do have to watch and look in the rearview mirror because sometimes there could be a truck behind us. The car behind us may be switching lanes, but your focus shouldn't be the review mirror. Your focus has got to be on the windshield going forward. It's quite hard to go forward when you're constantly looking back. Perception can shape your life, and you gain the ability to mold it any way you want.

Similarly, the cycle of life depends on your interpretations and how you take on a challenge. Difficulties and hurdles may pose a challenge, but tackling them with informed decisions and knowledge is how you will succeed. Similarly, poor communication often leads to poor management, which affects the child's behavior and upbringing. When we start a discussion, it's important to give your point of view with clear intentions. You should know what is the purpose of your words. What is your aim, and what outcome are you targeting? Relationships grow stronger when there is significant work done in regard to how you portray your words and what your target is. Assuming that you are right will lead you to be defensive. Have an open mind–in communicating only to win an argument will lead to the inability to grow and, in the long run, will be harmful to our relationships.

Often we are in a hurry to speak and to cover all the points in mind without giving the other person the opportunity to speak. With this approach, you may feel satisfied temporarily, but in the long run, it will waste your time and energy because the issue will remain. You might win arguments, but you will have disappointed individuals around you.

Reframe your emotions and see the difference. If you choose to be mellow when someone insults you and if you choose not to react to an insensitive comment made at you, you are in control. Sometimes, people will throw their "emotional garbage" at you, and you may not be able to get out of it. Therefore it is necessary to practice mindfulness. Also, think about the other person's perception and practice empathy. Dedicate a reason as to why the person may be feeling that way. Is it because of your actions or something you said?

Reasoning is the process of forming conclusions or sound judgments, and it is to think or argue in a logical manner. In the story I'm about to tell you, you will see the power of reasoning at work and how it created a positive outcome for both the child and the parents. I met a mom we'll call Mary at a workshop at which I spoke. She was very impressed with our organization, Fathers Forever, and had, from time to time, called me for advice about issues she was having with her ex-husband and co-parenting. About a week before Christmas, early in the morning, I received a phone call from Mary. She was angry, frantic, and on the verge of tears. It took me a few minutes to calm her down to get to the issues that had her so worked up. Mary had just had a serious disagreement with her ex-husband and vowed to fight him to the end on this issue. She declared that she was going to have the last word. The fight was about a Christmas present — yes, a Christmas present. That doesn't sound like something a couple should be fighting over, but these parents were fighting about it, and both parents promised to stand their ground.

Here was the problem: their 13-year-old son wanted a particular video game that contained scenes of gun violence. Mary was totally against him having it. Sam, the boy's father, didn't see anything wrong with his son having the video game; after all, it was just a game. There was no compromise in sight, and the 25th of December was approaching quickly. Mary and Sam had a couple of heated discussions. The most intense discussion had occurred the night before she called me. She was furious and hadn't gotten much sleep that night. Sam vowed to buy the $80 game for their son, and Mary vowed to put it in the trash can on Christmas day. She was calling to get my insight and opinion and probably to get me to co-sign on her decision. She said she had talked to a couple of her other friends, and they all agreed with her that she should stand her ground. But first, she wanted to know what I thought about it.

Well, I didn't agree with her decision, and I told her so in three points. First point: Sam had every right to buy his son the video game, even if the gift didn't meet her approval, as long as it didn't cause any imminent danger to their son. The silence on her end of the phone let me know that Mary did not particularly like this point. The second point I made was that she was about to start World War III if she threw an $80 game in the trash can, and the third point was they probably wouldn't have a merry Christmas this year. Mary took a deep breath as she asked me what she should do. My advice to her was to call the father, in a calm voice, and without getting into another heated argument, express her concerns about the video game. However, if Sam still disagreed with her, she had to respect his rights as a father. I suggested maybe she set some ground rules, one, that the game cannot be brought to her house, and if the son did bring the game to her house, she had every right to put it in the trash can. Later that day, she did have that conversation with Sam, who half-heartedly shrugged her off. But he was now aware of the consequences, and so was the son: if the game ended up in her house, it was going in the trash can. Problem solved (at least for now). Everybody was happy, and they did have a merry Christmas.

However, the problem was not completely solved. A few weeks later, the game did show up at Mary's house. She was not at all happy, and she did take it from their son, but just before she threw it in the trash, she called me to tell me what she was about to do. My advice was, "Yes, you have every right to make good on your promise." She had told both the father and the son the consequences of breaking her rule, which Sam had clearly broken. I suggested she take the video game away, but she shouldn't put it in the trash can. Rather, she should call Sam and make him aware that their son had violated the previously established rule. When she called Sam the next day, he was not at all happy with the son for bringing the game to his mother's home. He had a "come to Jesus" meeting with their son. Sam told the son the next time he carried the game to his mother's home, he would take it and throw it away himself. He also thanked Mary for not throwing the game away.

This time, the problem was solved, and the game never showed up at Mary's house again. One day a few months later, Mary asked their son about the game. He stated he lost interest in it not long after he got it, and gave it to one of his friends. There are two points from this story I want to emphasize. First, sometimes we have to stand and hold our ground during the battles we fight, but then sometimes, giving a little bit for the greater good is worth winning the war. Because of their already-strained relationship, the parents of this 13-year-old boy could've ended up in another major fight, but the powers of reasoning, compromise, and respect brought about a positive outcome. The impact of the video game itself faded in time, but the consequence of throwing away an $80 gift could have been the start of another battle that would have been lost by both parents and the son. The second point is that you must be careful about who you consult with. Make sure you have people around who may not always tell you what you want to hear but who will give you good, sound advice. The power of reasoning allowed love to win in this story.

Remember that your relationship with your child will largely depend on how well you have instilled ethics and values in their lives with your own actions as children tend to observe their elders. Work on your behavior by managing your thoughts and decide consciously whether you want to learn or just win for the sake of it. It's important to incorporate openness in your belief system. You should always believe that you have the courage to open up and share your feelings. No matter what, find a person who would listen to you. Once you have a strong relationship with your listener, have faith in them and trust their intentions. Similarly, the power of changing perspectives is an art that requires tedious amounts of patience.

REVISION TIME!

Q. 1. Please fill out the blanks with the most appropriate answer from the brackets.

a) Incorporate _____ with sincerity in your conversations. (oneness, openness, goodness, righteousness)

b) Make _____ and encourage using words instead of vindicating passive-aggressive behavior. (gossip, conversation, communication, small talk)

c) _____ can shape your life, and you gain the ability to mold it any way you want. (Dreaming, Driving, Perception, Drawing)

d) _____ is the process of forming conclusions or sound judgments, and it is to think or argue in a logical manner. (Calculating, Communicating, Reasoning, Drafting)

e) When we start a discussion, it's important to give your point of view with clear _____. (intentions, drama, excuses, possibilities)

Q. 2. Encircle 'True' or 'False' if you think the statements are right or wrong, respectively.

a) The cycle of life depends on your interpretations and how you take on a challenge.

True   False

b) When carrying out your responsibility as a parent, use your words and talk to your partner.

True   False

c) In order to instill excuses in your child's life, changing your perception is essential.

True   False

d) If you don't change your perception, you will continuously do the wrong thing, which will lead to constantly getting good results.

True   False

e) Good communication often leads to poor management, which affects the child's behavior and upbringing.

True   False

Q. 3. Describe in a single line what you have learned by reading this chapter.

_____

Q. 4. Describe in a single line how you will be applying what you have learned in this chapter.

_____

Answer Key

Q. 1. a) Incorporate <u>openness</u> with sincerity in your conversations.

b) Make <u>communication</u> and encourage using words instead of vindicating passive-aggressive behavior.

c) <u>Perception</u> can shape your life, and you gain the ability to mold it any way you want.

d) <u>Reasoning</u> is the process of forming conclusions or sound judgments, and it is to think or argue in a logical manner.

e) When we start a discussion, it's important to give your point of view with clear <u>intentions</u>.

Q. 2. a) True.

b) True.

c) False.

d) False.

e) False.

Q. 3 & 4. If you do not have an answer, reread the chapter and try to take a lesson from it. There is no right or wrong answer for these.

Chapter 8

Substance Abuse

Parents regularly engaging in substance abuse can cause
irreparable damage to their children.

Stephen King, an author, and screenwriter, who has been writing science-fiction, horror, and crime stories for decades, talked about substance abuse and how it is just a construct. He said, "The idea that the creative endeavor and mind-altering substances are entwined is one of the great pop-intellectual myths of our time." Stephen has explained that to think that creativity and taking drugs and alcohol are correlated is one the biggest misconceptions and only dulls our sensibility.

Substance abuse by a parent has damaging effects on their children as they tend to adopt these habits themselves when they grow up. Substance abuse has massive effects not only on the user but their family members as well. Children who witness their fathers battling addiction have disturbing effects on their emotional capabilities, which damages their intellectual upbringing. There are short-term and long-term effects of addiction as they inflict stress on peaceful and composed family life.

Alcohol and drug abuse causes conflict that weakens the bond of fathers with their children, and trust within the family begins to diminish. Children begin to put up walls around them as they become more conscious of the aggressive behavior that is inflicted by their fathers. Alcoholism and drug abuse may also lead to broken homes when the damage is irreparable, and communication becomes a hassle leading to a frustrating environment. As fathers are under the influence of alcohol, children endure their rage, mood swings, and an uneven temper which is quite unfair and unwarranted.

Fathers battling addiction also tend to abandon their children, which causes them distress and deep underlying trauma. When a child sees their father dealing with addiction, it tends to hinder their growth and delays their learning abilities. Children tend to learn from their environment and imitate their elders. According to a survey, children of alcoholic parents are more likely to abuse alcohol than children of non-alcoholic parents.

Children grow up feeling insecure and unsafe in a home where substance abuse prevails. As children are easily influenced by their father's attitude and behavior, they often blame themselves and believe they are the reason their father has chosen drugs and alcohol over them.

Addicted fathers have negative relations with their children as the flow of communication is full of disapproval and contempt. The environment overall is battered and radiates negativity whilst a positive outlook is largely negated. In these kinds of families, the only way a father remains relevant is by creating predicaments and problems. The toxic environment often makes the habit of substance abuse more solid.

Boundaries are often crossed, there is hardly any discipline in the house, and the family structure fails to pull through. Children tend to find themselves surrounded by misunderstandings as they are unable to decipher right from wrong. The repercussions that follow are that the children begin to rebel to gain their parents' attention and most often want some sanity amidst the whole frenzy. As there are no rules, children are unable to formulate their parent's responses in the future; therefore, they mold themselves according to their surroundings.

A sense of struggle prevails when a father is addicted to alcohol and drugs and sets the mood of the house as erratic, leading to issues of abandonment, fear, anxiety, and anger amongst his children. Such fathers often fail to recognize that they are alcoholics and tend to deny this fact when confronted. If a child points it out, they are addressed with anger and denial by the father.

When there is a lack of emotion present in a household, a father will opt for alcohol to suppress their thoughts and inhibitions, which leads to the anger being taken out on the children. Fathers tend to be overprotective and control their children's activities excessively when under the influence, as they deem their children as irresponsible and unable to look after themselves. Alcoholic people are insecure, and they tend to react without thinking because they don't want to recognize their emotions and feelings. An alcoholic father would sacrifice their morals and principles in order to dodge rejection by their children. Alcoholics are sensitive and often found to be disloyal to their family members.

Fathers with alcoholism never have the intention to harm their children deliberately, and sometimes, they don't even realize the kind of effect it is having on their children. When a father has an addiction and shows up at their child's school under the influence, it tends to embarrass the child, and it is sad and disheartening for them. At the age of 50, a person may forget what it felt like, but at the tender age of 7 or 8, it is disturbing.

A parent that suffers from drug and alcohol abuse severely affects a child's development and deeply impacts their overall stance toward life. In such an environment, the children often have the basic instinct to just survive, and the characteristics they tend to adapt are dysfunctional and uneven. Such characteristics often negatively impact future relationships, and the mental and physical health of such children tend to deteriorate.

A home that has an alcoholic father often has an impulsive and unpredictable environment. The kind of behavior and attitude inflicted by a father who has addiction tends to pass on to their children through verbal and non-verbal ways. There are often implicit and undeclared instructions that are practiced within the household. One of which is that no one is allowed to discuss substance abuse with anyone outside the family or even ask for help. In addition, there should be no discussion about feelings as an attempt to seek validation, which leads to a child never truly opening up.

Furthermore, there is a limitation on communication as parents' reaction is inconsistent; therefore, children tend to stay quiet as they are unable to decipher whether the response will be negative or positive. A child is made to believe that they are not good enough and made to work hard for their parents' approval, and if a child disagrees, they are labeled as egotistic and selfish.

Even when fathers carry out deleterious behavior, they expect their children to do the opposite and avoid any encounter that would upset their mood. There are restrictions placed on children from alcoholic homes; therefore, they tend to become accustomed to finding ways to make themselves safe. A child doesn't have an option as they are unable to choose for themselves, and thus, develop unhealthy patterns of behavior which leads to compromised mental health.

Children of alcoholic fathers tend to adopt traits that affect their psychological development and often have these traits in order to cope with the aggression inflicted on them in the past. Such children do not deem themselves as trustworthy and treat others with suspicion. In addition to that, they tend to be overly sensitive when someone remarks or comments on their lifestyle. Additionally, such children are high achievers, opt for perfection, and tend to think of others before helping themselves. Such children fail to recognize their own feelings when they are adults and remove themselves from situations that involve confrontation. Children of fathers battling with addiction tend to take in and accept bad behavior from others also and have no sense of respect for themselves.

Since children of alcoholic parents have restricted resources and are left on their own, they have no idea how to deal with stress leading to struggles in expressing emotions and feelings. With observation and prior knowledge of how fathers have behaved during important milestones such as forgetting birthdays or missing their graduation ceremonies, children tend to believe that they should not put faith in anyone, especially their parents.

A father's passive-aggressive behavior toward their children makes them fearful and afraid, which leads to concealing their actual thoughts and worries. Therefore, such children grow up feeling caged and see freedom as an alien concept. As a father denies their substance abuse, children are scared to discuss anything important in their lives with them as well. A father constantly denying that he has a drug problem will also invalidate their child's life choices.

Children from compromised homes are indecisive and find it difficult to make friends or make the right decisions for themselves. It is fairly difficult to explain alcoholism to children in a way that they are able to comprehend what it actually is. Yet, it is important to recognize that children understand more by observing. It is vital to highlight to a child that substance abuse by their parents is not the child's fault and a parent is not their responsibility. A child must be allowed to ask as many questions as they want and be able to get honest answers. A child with alcoholic parents can be recognized for erratic and defensive behavior in school, failing grades, and so on.

Even though many children are able to cope and exercise strength, others may not have the circumstances, or choice, to branch out and vent. Such children tend to develop depression, anxiety, and even a drinking habit themselves at a young age. Children often ask themselves why their parents drink too much which often leads them to inadequate answers and leaves them to wonder.

A person may consume alcohol to feel relaxed and calm at first, but if this practice is continued for a long time, there comes a time when they are unable to suppress their urge to drink and stop themselves. It takes a lot of determination and self-control to battle addiction. Substance abuse causes massive cravings to consume drugs and alcohol as it affects the brain and makes changes in it, causing a yearning to be under the influence. Being sober becomes an impossible task to achieve, yet to recover is one of the greatest things you can do for your children.

No matter how many times a parent has failed or had a relapse, they must pick themselves up and try once again to fix their addiction. The situation may seem hopeless and out of hand, yet it is crucial to support and make changes in your lifestyle for the sake of your children. The first sign of recovery is that you have identified that there is a problem of addiction in your life, and you are prepared to make the necessary alteration.

To get sober, it is important to eradicate the people who accentuate and encourage drinking. Also, it is important to recognize how a parent deals with tension and what kind of perception they have for themselves. It is common to feel disruptive and conflicted when giving up a substance, yet it is important to remember that it is the root cause of all the problems. Fathers have to administer a lot of motivation and support from within themselves. Once they commit to change, they will be able to kick off their addiction and reclaim control over their life.

To take the initial step to recovery, it is important that fathers remind themselves of why they are quitting and what went wrong with the previous attempts at recovery. It is important to set goals that are realistic and achievable, such as trying to limit the consumption slowly and day by day. There might be withdrawal symptoms, yet it is important to pull through. It is vital to remove all kinds of stressors that remind a person of their addiction, such as workplace, home, and other areas. Asking family and friends for support is also a step to recovery, as asking for their help in the commitment to recovery may boost a father's confidence.

It is important to recognize that every person takes treatment differently, and everyone's needs are not the same. When there is a treatment offered to a father, it should address more than just substance abuse. Relationships, health, career, and all the essential factors that surround a person are affected. Successful treatment involves a new type of living situation as compared to before and recognizes the reasons a father has opted for substance abuse. When a father quits, they must stay committed and get a follow-up after every few months just to make sure they stay on track.

The more addictive and intense the substance abuse, the longer it will take for the process of healing. After recognizing addiction and seeking treatment, it is important to incorporate healthy ways to deal with stress and point out the reasons for substance abuse. Was it to deal with anxiety, was it due to painful past experiences or losing in an argument?

When fathers become confident in their abilities to cope, they tend to practice their ability to de-stress, due to which the feelings of unsettlement take a backseat. To avoid substance abuse, a father must look after themselves physically, such as work out regularly, go for a spa day, and whatever they feel relaxed doing. Sometimes, picturing a scenic beauty with their eyes closed just to feel peaceful and calm also helps. Deep breathing also calms down a person while enjoying the aroma of coffee beans or fresh flowers. It is important to incorporate movement and go out to enjoy the breeze and savor the sun.

Triggers and cravings should be monitored during the path to recovery so they can be avoided. The most important aspect is maintaining the urges and impulses. The mind needs a lot of time and energy to replace those connections that led a person to their downfall. It is important to avoid places such as clubs and bars that would prompt the addiction. Rebuilding past relationships that were destroyed due to substance abuse is key to recovery as well.

It is significant to divulge all the details of addiction and be completely honest about the substance abuse behavior when seeking medical treatment. There is no need to feel ashamed or be conscious as the path to recovery has been carved, and there shouldn't be anything holding a person back. Moreover, to avoid cravings, a father must take part in activities that distract them, such as spending time with their children playing ball or helping with their homework, etc.

It is important to talk about the addiction as it helps mellow down its effects and reduces the desire to abuse drugs and alcohol. It is important to change the perception about alcohol as positive affirmations toward it may lead to a relapse. It is crucial to make a list of the negative repercussions, such as failing in a relationship or getting fired from work as the outcome of substance abuse. This will set a reminder that abusing drugs and alcohol will not make a person feel better except giving a temporary high, which leads to dire consequences in the long run.

It is the duty of parents to keep themselves in check for signs of substance abuse. If a parent has been drinking in the daytime, they should recognize that it is an unhealthy sign. Also, selling stuff from the house to pay for alcohol is also a sign of addiction. Taking lunch money from the children and using child support money to pay for drugs and alcohol is also a sign of substance abuse.

It is important to identify these signs and consider

151

them as life-altering problems. It is vital to get help from a professional and recover from the addiction as it will be beneficial for the family in the long run. It leads to a healthy environment and an overall functional family dynamic. The path to recovery is as difficult as the addiction as the first few months will be hard to manage, but it is important to remember that the results, in the end, will benefit the whole family.

Providing a stable home for the children should be a father's top priority, and there should be sufficient guidance from the therapist that you have chosen to help you recover. A father must maintain an environment that exuberates stability and includes customs and traditions that should be followed routinely. There need to be conversations between a father and his children with the assurance that there is a circle of mutual trust and respect.

Children tend to feel uneasy when there is an absence of feelings or lack of honest discussions and, as a result, do not trust themselves and their vision. It is important to hold thoughtful and honest conversations with children so that they will be able to name their feelings and put words to what they are actually going through.

Let me tell you a story about the significance of

building a strong relationship between a father and son and how it deepens the bond after the father becomes sober.

I met with a grandfather in my office one day—let's call him Tom — who shared an amazing story with me. Tom's story points out the wisdom of an elderly man who helped his son, Herbert, without saying a word. His actions spoke louder than his words. Herbert and his girlfriend, Helen, had a baby. A few years later, the relationship ended, and after a couple of more years, the couple started having co-parenting issues. They ended up in family court, where an agreement was reached that Herbert was to get his son every weekend, and Helen was to have him during the week because of the child's school schedule. During the summer months, Herbert would have him during the week and then Helen would have him each weekend. They both loved their son and had been doing a good job of managing joint custody of him.

A few months later, Helen found a job and moved back to her hometown. Now, Helen and their son lived about 70 miles from Herbert. The parents agreed to meet halfway to drop off and pick up their son. This strategy worked out well for the first couple of months until Helen started having transportation issues. She didn't have a driver's license, and the person who was providing her transportation got a new job, which presented a scheduling conflict. Herbert decided he wasn't going to drive 70 miles each way every weekend to get his son. He felt that this new situation wasn't fair as, according to the initial agreement, Helen was to meet him halfway. Herbert felt that Helen needed to do her part regardless of her circumstances.

After a couple of weekends, Tom, the grandfather, noticed his grandson wasn't at family dinners and functions, so he asked Herbert why he wasn't getting his grandson every weekend as agreed. Herbert stated Helen had transportation issues, she couldn't meet him halfway, and he wasn't going to drive 70 miles each way twice every weekend because it wasn't fair to him. Herbert stressed that the agreement said she was supposed to meet him halfway, and she needed to do her part again regardless of her circumstances. Tom told Herbert that seeing his son every weekend was more important than fighting over transportation.

Tom even offered to help with gas, but Herbert rejected his father's advice and vowed not to drive 70 miles twice a week; it just wasn't fair. He stated it wasn't his fault that she didn't have transportation. The next weekend, Tom had an idea. He told Herbert he was going to be out of town, and on the way back, he would pick up his grandson and bring him for a visit. Herbert agreed. Helen was contacted, and the son was delivered to his father. What a reunion it was! The two were so happy to see each other, and they couldn't stop hugging and giving each other high fives. They were inseparable all weekend. Tom also agreed to take his grandson back home, and he did.

For the next two months, Tom drove the 140-mile roundtrip every weekend, picked up his grandson for visits with Herbert, and returned him to Helen. Tom never said a word about why he was doing this, but eventually, Herbert got the message: his son was worth driving 70 miles twice each weekend. One weekend, Herbert called Tom and said, "Dad, I got him this weekend." Tom told me that three years later, Herbert is still going strong with his weekend drives. Did the father love his son? Of course, he did, but his love for his son was not enough at the beginning of this story. He went many months without seeing his son, whom he said he loved very much.

The grandfather, in his wisdom, took action to create a path that allowed the father to see the error of his ways. The father did finally see and corrected his mistake. This story had a happy ending. Unfortunately, many such stories don't end this well; in those cases, the parents' love for their children is not enough to overcome transportation or the hundreds of other issues that interrupt strong parent-child relationships.

REVISION TIME!

Q. 1. Please fill out the blanks with the most appropriate answer from the brackets.

a) Children who witness their father battling _____ have disturbing effects on their emotional capabilities and damages their intellectual upbringing. (addiction, atrocity, anatomy, agreement)

b) Since children of alcoholic parents have _____ resources and are left on their own, they have no idea how to deal with stress leading to struggles in expressing emotions and feelings. (unlimited, restricted, uncanny, demanding)

c) Fathers with alcoholism never have the intention to _____ their children deliberately, and sometimes they don't even realize the kind of effect it has on their children. (love, harm, scold, disturb)

d) A parent that suffers from drug and alcohol abuse severely affects a child's _____ and deeply impacts their overall stance toward life. (destiny, life, school, development)

e) A sense of struggle prevails when a father is addicted to alcohol and drugs and sets the mood of the house as erratic, leading to issues of _____, fear, anxiety, and anger amongst his children. (confrontation, abandonment, security, directness)

Q. 2. Encircle 'True' or 'False' if you think the statements are right or wrong, respectively.

a) A person may drink alcohol to feel relaxed and calm, yet there comes a time when they are unable to suppress their urge to drink and stop themselves.

  True   False

b) A home that has an alcoholic father often has a calm and peaceful environment.

  True   False

c) Children grow up feeling secure and safe in a home where substance abuse prevails.

  True   False

d) A child is made to believe that they are not good enough and made to work hard for their parents' approval, and if a child disagrees, they are labeled as egotistic and selfish.

  True   False

e) Substance abuse by a parent has damaging effects on their children as they tend to adopt these habits themselves when they grow up.

     True   False

Q. 3. Describe in a single line what you have learned by reading this chapter.

_____

Q. 4. Describe in a single line how you will be applying what you have learned in this chapter.

_____

Answer Key

Q. 1. a) Children who witness their father battling <u>addiction</u> have disturbing effects on their emotional capabilities and damages their intellectual upbringing.

b) Since children of alcoholic parents have <u>restricted</u> resources and are left on their own, they have no idea how to deal with stress, leading to struggles in expressing emotions and feelings.

c) Fathers with alcoholism never have the intention to <u>harm</u> their children deliberately, and sometimes, they don't even realize the kind of effect it has on their children.

d) A parent who suffers from drug and alcohol abuse severely affects a child's <u>development</u> and deeply impacts their overall stance toward life.

e) A sense of struggle prevails when a father is addicted to alcohol and drugs and sets the mood of the house as erratic, leading to issues of <u>abandonment</u>, fear, anxiety, and anger amongst his children.

Q. 2. a) True.

b) False.

c) False.

d) True.

e) True.

Q. 3 & 4. If you do not have an answer, reread the chapter and try to take a lesson from it. There is no right or wrong answer for these.

Chapter 9

Domestic Violence

Abusers often claim they lost control, but the fact is, they abuse to gain control.

Dr. Sarvesh Jain, a philosopher and critically acclaimed author from India, talked about domestic violence and how inflicting pain on the vulnerable is not a sign of strength. He said, "Raising your hand to the powerless is no act of manliness." Jain has referred to toxic masculinity as a sign of weakness, saying that an individual's manhood is not defined by taking advantage of the helpless.

Domestic violence isn't just physical abuse but behaviors and actions that tend to exercise power and gain control over a partner or spouse. It is devastating for children exposed to domestic violence as they tend to feel guilt-ridden and entirely blame themselves for it. When children witness domestic violence at home, it affects their confidence and leaves a mark on their personalities. Such children often have difficulty falling asleep; they become more whiny and sensitive and adopt habits such as thumb-sucking and stuttering. Children are horrified when they see their parents abusing each other; this takes a toll on them and their wellbeing. They try to hide their emotions and put a brave face in front of the world, but their state of mind is ultimately reflected when they get terrible grades or refuse to participate in school activities.

Women have been subjected to domestic violence by men for centuries through mental abuse, such as insults and hurtful words, and physical abuse, such as being kicked and beaten. Domestic violence is the number one cause of injury to women between the ages of 15 - 44 in the U.S., more than car accidents, muggings and rapes combined. (Uniform Crime Reports, Federal Bureau of Investigation, 1991.) Of the women murdered each year in the U.S., 30% are killed by their current or former husbands or boyfriends. (Violence Against Women: Estimates from the Redesigned Survey, U.S. Department of Justice, Bureau of Justice Statistics, August 1995.)

About 95% of known victims of relationship violence are females who are abused by their male partners. (Straus, M.A., and Gelles, R.J. (eds), Physical Violence in American Families, Transaction Publishers, New Brunswick, NJ. 1990.)

Children who witness abuse in their homes are most likely to repeat the cycle and tend to abuse their future partners when they grow old, as they consider it a norm. Abusive fathers also tend to inflict violence on their children as well. 50% of men who frequently abuse their wives also abuse their children. (Stacy, W. and Schupe, A., The Family Secret, Beacon Press, Boston, MA, 1983.) A child who lives in a family where there is violence between parents is 15 times more likely to be abused. (L, Bergman, "Dating violence among high school students," Social Work 37 (1), 1992.)

I, fortunately, have not been a personal recipient of this, or never have I abused someone, but a lot of my friends, family members, and coworkers have been victims of domestic violence. Children raised in abusive households suffer greatly as adults; they tend to develop mental health problems like anxiety and depression, and anger issues.

The movie 'The Burning Bed' tells the story of an abuser's wife. The woman's husband would beat her every weekend after getting drunk, and the police would come to her rescue and take her statement, but the woman would never press charges. This happened for months until the woman couldn't take it anymore, so one day after her husband passed out due to being intoxicated, she tied him to the bed, threw gasoline over him, and set the bed on fire. The woman burned the house down and her husband with it.

She was arrested and charged with premeditated murder. When she went to trial, her lawyer presented the evidence and showed the police records that verified that she was abused for months; and suggested she temporarily lost it. The woman actually won the case, and domestic violence took a turn because of this movie. Many Hollywood celebrities, news organizations, mothers against domestic violence, and non-profit organizations started talking about it and the devastating effect it had on our community and our children.

Earlier, women wouldn't press charges, and the police couldn't do anything about it, but now the laws have changed. If the police find evidence of abuse, they will arrest the abuser, take them downtown, and put a domestic violence charge against them. All in all, the law has changed, and it came out of the movie 'The Burning Bed.'

If someone is abusive to their partner, that's domestic violence. Often, people don't consider verbal abuse as part of domestic violence, but it is a part of it nonetheless, along with physical and mental abuse. Anytime you put your hands on somebody and try to control and manipulate them, whether you leave any physical injury or not, you're holding them against their will.

Domestic violence is like a power surge as the thing that's supposed to be empowering your family, which is a father, is the very thing that's destroying the family.

The worst kind of violence is when you no longer feel secure in your home, which is supposed to be your safe haven, as the person who tells you that they love you is the very person who abuses you. You have to watch that very person, your father, who is supposed to empower you, destroy your life.

Abusers often claim they can't control their anger, so they tend to take it out on their family members. They have anger issues, not because they can't control it, but they choose not to control it. The fact is that abusers are usually not out of control; they do it to gain power and control over the other person. They often use a series of tactics besides violence, including threats, intimidation, psychological abuse, and isolation, to control their partners. (Straus, M.A., Gelles R.J. & Steinmetz, S., Behind Closed Doors, Anchor Books, NY, 1980.)

People who are abused often blame themselves for it, as some women say it's their fault that their partner got mad in the first place. They blame themselves for the man's behavior.

166

Most people who are abused blame themselves for causing the violence. (Barnett, Martinex, Keyson, "The relationship between violence, social support, and self-blame in battered women," Journal of Interpersonal Violence, 1996.)

However, it is not right to assume that only women could fall victim to domestic violence. Sometimes, it is the other way around. We don't hear about it, but it happens more often than we know. It is because sometimes the men are embarrassed to report that a woman is abusing them. Manipulating their partner into thinking that they are responsible for the abuse and deserve to be treated that way makes the abuser feel in control. They feel a surge of satisfaction that this surge of power brings along.

Most people wonder that if a woman is getting beaten every other day and getting slapped around, why is she still standing there? Why hasn't she left? It's because she has a fear for her life and children. There are several complicated reasons why it is difficult for a person to leave an abusive partner; a common one is fear - women who leave abusers are at a 75% greater chance of getting killed by the abuser than those who stay. (U.S. Department of Justice, Bureau of Justice Statistics National Crime Victimization Survey, 1995.) An abuser is generally abusive to the people around his professional life as well, and when their victims see the kind of person who isn't afraid of anyone, they tend to wallow in self-pity, get frightened and avoid coming out of their cage of powerlessness.

As a man, what would you do if you find out that your daughter or sister, or mom was involved in an abusive relationship? What would you do with the abuser? How would you respond to that? You will try to find a way to bring your loved ones to safety and protect them. For a man to put his hands on a woman and abuse his power is uncalled for. We need men to make sure that they're putting a stop to this and not participating in any forms of abuse. They have to find other ways to express their anger besides beating up their loved ones.

Examine yourself and see, what are you doing as a man? How are you expressing your anger? Are you abusing your family? Are you abusing your loved ones? It doesn't have to be physical to be called abuse. Verbal abuse is just as powerful as physical abuse. Do you curse your children out for not listening to you? For not following everything you say and having opinions, ideas, and plans of their own? When you yell at them, scold or curse them out, it makes them feel small and unwanted.

Once, I was walking down the stairs of my apartment, and I saw this guy with these two beautiful little girls, five or six years old, who were twins. They were walking down the steps and doing what children do. Their father was behind them and was yelling, screaming, and calling them every name in the book, and I'm thinking, how can you do that as a father to your little kid? I mean, what possessed you to even think about doing something like that? This is your flesh and blood. This is what you produced and for you to do that is an injustice.

There is very little social support for women who are battered, and it plays a negative role in their psychological wellbeing. As the abuser is controlling and sometimes even restricting the victim's movement, there is a slight chance that they can find support from their family and peers. Victims who do manage to share their feelings and extend their issues with their support system have a lower risk of falling into depression.

When a pregnant woman faces domestic violence, the birth of the child is affected and, in some severe cases, it affects the health of the child even before they are born. Women tend to visit their physicians more as they feel the trauma of abuse is affecting their children. Pregnant victims often have miscarriages when abuse is hurled at them and blamed by the abuser for losing the child.

Children who intervene during the fights to protect their mothers are abused by their fathers as well. The emotional labor of watching your mother get battered and bruised tends to disrupt the mental peace and stability of a child. The child is confused between helping the victim and pretending they didn't see anything as it may result in the abuser hitting the child as well. Witnessing your mother getting abused inflicts the same amount of pain as being abused yourself, which is traumatizing.

To lessen the effects of domestic violence on a family, there needs to be an intervention at the right time. A physician should get involved in referring them to a family therapist. Women and their children tend to develop Post-Traumatic Stress Disorder (PTSD) and find it difficult to cope unless there is professional care provided to them. Children from domestic abuse households tend to have an aggressive personality, lack social skills, have anxiety and fears. They tend to exhibit a lack of trust in others and perceive the world as dangerous, intimidating, and unsafe.

When a therapist is talking to a child, they should expedite an environment that is open, non-judgmental, and empathetic. A child should be freely able to discuss their feelings and talk about the incidents that have taken place in their home. The therapist should be helpful and direct the child to cope with the violence by reframing their thought process. If the violence continues, it will be difficult for the child to completely let go of their inhibitions and recover from the abuse they witnessed or went through.

Children need an environment that is safe and stable. Children have the right to have a home where they feel secure and where their elders are present for them in moments of happiness as well as challenges—an adult who will protect and shelter them from all kinds of harm. Children need regularity and normalcy in their day-to-day life, which is beneficial for their emotional intelligence and physical development. A child should be aware that there are others means of solving problems apart from violence and an open discussion is key between parents and their children.

"Violence can come from anywhere, at any time, but the worst kind is when it comes from within the home, from an immediate family member."

The term "in harm's way" means in the path of danger, harm, injury, and even death. To put someone in harm's way means that one person is liable for putting another person on the path of danger, harm, injury, or death. We understand how this works in times of war. The Commander-In-Chief orders soldiers into battle, and when they are sent in to fight the enemy, the soldiers are definitely put in harm's way. They are put in the path of danger, harm, injury, and even death. Wars are sometimes deemed necessary, but there is another war that is raging in our society and communities that is so totally UNNECESSARY. It is our children and families who are put in harm's way.

I am referring to the battle of domestic violence, which is carried out by people who say these three magic words: "I love you." Yet, their actions of violence speak louder than their language of love. I guess this is an appropriate time to say that in such a situation, love is not enough. Consider this story, "Power Surge," which I wrote and shared in my first book 'Chat and Chew.' A power surge is a sudden increase in voltage sent back into the system it once powered, thus, destroying the system. Lightning strikes are a common cause of power surges, but for the most part, a power surge comes from inside the home because of an electrical shortage. This phenomenon sounds a lot like domestic violence.

Violence can come from anywhere, at any time, but the worst kind is when it comes from an immediate family member (an emotional shortage) in the home. In one of our Fathers Forever domestic violence classes, I asked, "How many fathers have ever had a D.V. charge?" To my surprise, over half of the guys raised their hands. Some fathers stated they were set up by their partners, while others admitted to their abusive behavior. One particular father said, "You have to hit her every now and again to keep her in line." I asked him to please explain. His response was disturbing, to say the least, although I had heard it before. He said he grew up in an abusive household where his father beat his mother, his siblings, and him, often for no apparent reason. "He would get mad and fuss for a few days, then 'flip out' and begin beating us, starting with my Mom. After the beatings, he would be very nice, buying us things, helping my Mom in the kitchen, and he would later apologize but say that it was our fault and that he had to keep us in line. Things would be normal for a while, but in a few months, or sometimes, weeks, the fussing would start up again."

I asked him how he felt about what happened in his home, and he said, "I knew it was wrong, but it did keep us in line, including my Mom. She didn't talk back to him as much for a while after the beatings." He then said he tried it a few times in his own home, and that's how he got the domestic violence charge.

Lenore Walker created "The Cycle of Abuse" model, in which she identified four phases of abuse.

Phase 1 — Tension Building;

Phase 2 — Acting Out (the abuse);

Phase 3 — Reconciliation or the Honeymoon;

Phase 4 — The Calm.

We saw that pattern pretty clearly in this father's story. I instructed each father to go home, take his partner's hand, and, palm-to-palm, measure to see how much bigger his hand is compared to hers. Then, arm wrestle her and see how much more strength he has over her. I went on to explain one of the reasons men are bigger and stronger is to protect their women and children. Anything else is an abuse of power. No family member should ever be put in harm's way by another family member; yet, there are millions of children in our society who have been put in harm's way every day by family members while in the comfort of their homes. When those children grow up to be adults, some repeat that same behavior and abuse their children. Their children are put in harm's way as well, and the cycle continues.

A few years ago, I was invited to speak at a conference. An agency was showing how they had saved a woman and her children from their abusive husband and stepfather. They provided "Wrap-around Services," which included relocation, counseling, and employment assistance for the mother. They really had done a great job! Then I posed a question, "What services did you offer the husband/father?" To my surprise, none; except a jail cell, of course. He would be released one day but with a criminal record, which would hinder him in finding a job. So, he would find another family to abuse, and again the cycle would continue.

We need surge protectors! A surge protector is a device that contains circuitry that prevents damage from reaching the electrical equipment plugged into it when a storm causes a power surge to occur. I often wonder why there aren't more programs to help men understand the root causes of their behavior that leads them to domestic violence. The father mentioned earlier, perhaps like many other fathers, has an emotional shortage. He has a distorted view of his role as a man and a father. We, as a society, need to put more surge protectors — services for men — in our communities.

If we are going to stop domestic violence, we have to provide programs for both the victims and the perpetrators. Yes, they have to go to jail for their cowardly acts and abuse of power, but they should be treated as well. A community with few or no services to aid men in understanding domestic violence — their emotional shortage— and its effects is like a home without a surge protector: both can suffer from the abuse of power. So when will love be enough to keep parents from abusing — breaking — their children? If we say we love them, then we must not put them in the path of danger, harm, injury, and even death by way of domestic violence, whether it is physical, emotional, or mental.

We, as a community, have to BOTH demand and provide treatment, rehabilitation, and support for the perpetrators to keep our children out of harm's way. Yes, we must tell our children and families many times each and every day that we love them, but that declaration must be supported with a safe environment, free from any abuse and inappropriate behavior. This includes abusive and inappropriate actions from relatives and friends who live in or visit our homes. As Elizabeth Stone wrote, "Making the decision to have a child is momentous. It is to decide forever to have your heart go walking around outside your body." If our behaviors as parents reflected that quote, then love will ALWAYS be enough to keep our children and families out of harm's way.

REVISION TIME!

Q. 1. Please fill out the blanks with the most appropriate answer from the brackets.

a) Raising your hand to the _____ is no act of manliness. (strong, coward, powerless, vulnerable)

b) Domestic violence isn't just _____ abuse but behaviors and actions that tend to exercise power and gain control over a partner or spouse. (creating, physical, trauma, inflicting)

c) About _____ of known relationship violence are females who are abused by their male partners. (65%, 45%, 85%, 95%)

d) 50% of men who frequently abuse their wives also frequently abuse their _____. (co-workers, peers, children, staff)

e) When an abuse victim sees the kind of person who isn't afraid of anyone, they tend to wallow in self-pity, get frightened and never come out of their _____ of powerlessness. (box, cage, circle, drive)

Q. 2. Encircle 'True' or 'False' if you think the statements are right or wrong, respectively.

a) Children who see abuse happening in their homes are most likely to repeat the cycle and tend to abuse their future partners when they grow old.

True   False

b) There is a lot of social support for women who are battered and it plays a negative role in a women's psychological wellbeing.

True   False

c) Domestic violence is not just only men beating the women, but it's also women beating men.

True   False

d) The abuse of power makes the abuser feel in control and feel a surge of satisfaction after they have hit their significant other.

True   False

e) People who abuse are usually out of control; they do it to gain power and control over the other person.

True   False

Q. 3. Describe in a single line what you have learned by reading this chapter.

Q. 4. Describe in a single line how you will be applying what you have learned in this chapter.

_____

Answer Key

Q. 1. (a) Raising your hand to the <u>powerless</u> is no act of manliness.

b) Domestic violence isn't just <u>physical</u> abuse but behaviors and actions that tend to exercise power and gain control over a partner or spouse.

c) About <u>95%</u> of known victims of relationship violence are females who are abused by their male partners.

d) 50% of men who frequently abuse their wives also frequently abuse their <u>children</u>.

e) When a woman sees the kind of person who isn't afraid of anyone, they tend to wallow in self-pity, get frightened and never come out of their <u>cage</u> of powerlessness.

Q. 2. a) True.

b) False.

c) True.

d) True.

e) False.

Q. 3 & 4. If you do not have an answer, reread the chapter and try to take a lesson from it. There is no right or wrong answer for these.

Chapter 10

Destiny Development, Part 1

If we are all born with gifts and talents in us, then it's within ourselves to pursue them.

William Shakespeare, a famous playwright, actor, and poet, once said, "It is not in the stars to hold our destiny but in ourselves." We are in control of our lives, and the journey might be a struggle, but when you reach the end goal, it will be worth it.

Life is really about dreams, gifts, and talents, and being able to identify them in yourself will help you identify the talents in your children. Sometimes, there might be barriers that will keep you from walking into your gifts and talents. Let me tell you a story about a man, let's call him Tim, who went to a massive warehouse with all kinds of boxes, from small to medium to large. Tim went up to the counter and asked for all kinds of things such as longevity and money, and the guy behind the countertop gave him box after box, which was everything that Tim desired.

Tim asked the man, "So what's in all these boxes?" And he said, "Everything that you asked me to give to you, I just gave it to you, but I gave it to you in a seed form. You have to take that seed, plant it, nurture it and make it grow." The point is, God gives us all the talent and ability and what we have to do is take that seed, plant it, nurture it and watch it grow.

We all saw Michael Jordan or Tiger Woods and many other athletes and learned how they became talented and owned their gifts. We watched them dunk, slam dunk, and put a little white ball in small holes, sometimes a hundred feet away, but what we didn't see is what went on behind the scenes, where they're practicing day in and day out. We think it's not that difficult, and those athletes are gifted, believing that talent just comes naturally. However, the truth is, they had to work hard to polish and enhance the skills they possessed. You have to practice and water that seed for it to bear the fruit. Then you have to recognize the gifts given to you by God and detect the skills and talents that your child may possess.

Start to recognize that you do have a talent and a gift, and you have something that you can offer. You need to have courage and confidence. Confidence is knowing, courage is doing. You start to be who you are, which builds confidence.

You start to do what you need to do, which is the courage to get your talents and gifts out in the world.

Here's another story, 'Sweet Over Stink,' but let me start off with a quote, "Don't let your talent and your ability be absorbed by your character flaws. Ultimately, it's a matter of integrity." Growing up, my mom would tell us to go wash, take a bath and do the things we need to do to stay clean. We would go to the bathroom, pretend like we were washing, and we wouldn't put soap on. We'd just put a little water on our arms and come out two minutes later. My mom would think that we washed up, and about an hour later, when we would come by her, she'd smell the odor from our underarms. She'd instantly know we didn't wash up, and she would call us back and say, "You didn't take a bath." All we did was put on deodorant. Well, I call it sweet over stink. Our underarms would be smelly, and so we'd try to put the deodorant on to mask the smell, but it won't last very long.

We see a lot of musicians, and they're very gifted and talented, but their character flaws consist of alcohol and drugs. That's a character flaw that may ruin their lives and even end up killing them and their gifts. There are many people who I wish were still here because their talent and abilities were amazing, but their character flaws took them away from us too soon.

What does the word integrity mean? Oftentimes, people use it to talk about character flaws, but originally, it comes from the word Integra, which is about being structured. So what structure do you have in your life that's keeping you on track? What truth do you have in your life that's keeping you on track? Because if you don't have those, there is a lack of structure there. When a building collapses, people go in, and they try to find out what caused the collapse. As, sometimes, people cut corners; where they're supposed to put in four by four posts, they put two by four, which is less compared to the amount of concrete required to keep the building intact. Labors use that amount of concrete, but you really can't see that because the walls are there, and they're right up. The integrity of the building was compromised because somebody did some things that they shouldn't have done, and the weight that's supposed to hold up this structure collapsed.

Look at that as a character flaw because if you don't have your character in order, you won't be able to take the weight of life. You will get corrupt and, eventually, explode. You will collapse, and your children will be the victims of your lack of integrity or your lack of character. Put out the structure of who you are, and use your gifts and talents to make way through life. When you're trying to lead your family, you have to be strong yourself.

I asked a lot of people what, according to them, is the richest place in the city? And the people say the bank and similar places, but it is actually the graveyards because a lot of people die with their gifts unutilized. People have them, they're in there, but they didn't do anything with it. Don't be that person who died before realizing the gift they had because they couldn't identify what they were. You can't help out your children and show them the right direction they need to go if you don't know it yourself.

One of the stories that I often recall is 'The Value Was the Same.' I know we've all been beaten up in life and have made some poor choices. We made mistakes and did some things that we can look back and say weren't good. But how do you learn and get over them? How do you move forward? I was walking down the street one day, and as I looked down on the ground, there were beat-up nickels and a couple of pennies there. It was a rainy day, so I reached down and picked those nickels up and put them in my pocket. Later, I went into a store, bought what I was going to buy, got to the cash register, and gave some cash.

The cashier needed some change, so I reached in my pocket and pulled out the same nickels I had picked up earlier. I gave it to the cashier, she put the money in the cash register and went on about her business. It was then that this thought came to me about 'the value of the same.' I thought, wow, this rusted nickel was left out in the elements. I don't know how long it had been there. Maybe it just got there or had been there for weeks, days, or even months. I don't know. But that nickel with just as worthy, and it was the same as compared to a shiny nickel. The lady didn't say, "Oh, this is beaten up. I can't take it." She put it in a drawer that day, and that nickel got back into the circulation of life.

The point is, you may have some things in your life that went wrong, but your value is still the same. You're still worthy of who God made you to be, and you haven't lost your value at all; neither have you lost your gifts and talents. Get back up and get back into the struggle of life. The Federal Reserve made the nickel durable to take all the elements of life. Yes, it's been beaten up. It's been bruised. It was discolored, but its value remained the same; the same goes for you. Yes. You've been beaten up, but your value is the same. You haven't lost who you are.

God created you, made you this person, and gave you

gifts, talents, and abilities, and it is up to you how you utilize it for your own good and for your child.

Let me tell you another story. I was traveling to Orlando, Florida, a few years ago as a friend of mine invited me to come over and be a part of a round table discussion. We discussed some things, and after my flight, I went to get my baggage claim, but it was not there. When we lose our baggage, we all think something bad has happened. My baggage was lost, and I flipped out. I frustrated the lady standing at the desk as I asked her multiple times, "How could you lose my baggage? How could you lose my stuff?"

I was only traveling with my essentials, and they got lost. So, naturally, I flipped out, filed a report, and yelled at them for losing my belongings. I was not happy at all. I was there with two or three other people who had also lost their luggage. They told us to come back after four or five hours. They promised that baggage would be there or they would deliver them, but I said no and that I'll come get it. I told them to call me and let me know when the flight gets there, and I'll be there. Lo and behold, I got a call, I picked up my baggage, and everything was there. I was so happy that the complaint didn't happen, and all my anger went away because I had my baggage. The point is, the people you choose to travel with in your life are your baggage; your kids and your family are a part of it.

There are times that we don't even know that we've left our loved ones behind. Just like I didn't know my baggage wasn't there until I got to my destination. Your loved ones are your baggage. Those are the ones you chose to live with and build your life around. Maybe it wasn't your fault that your relationship with your partner didn't work out. Maybe you and your children couldn't see eye to eye before, or maybe you didn't make an effort to understand their goals and plans or get along with them. However, now is the time for you. Go and claim your baggage; go claim the stuff that belongs to you; after all, you are the one who chose it. Help them develop their gifts, talents, and abilities. Don't let your character flaws get in the way or stop you from helping them be what they were created to do.

Empower your relationships by being the first to apologize. There are things that you can do to get back on track and if you're not there already, forgive and move on. Let go of all of those things that can stand in your way of being free and being the person you want to be. One of the highest honors that you can have as a father and as a man is to take care of your children, be responsible, and forget about everything that happened in the past. Promise yourself that from that day forward, you're going to make sure your kids know they have a father who loves them.

This is one of my quotes, "No doubt, both parents love their children, but sometimes, their perception about the other parent casts a shadow on their love and prevents them from being the loving parents they were destined to be."

I love stories, as you can see; check this one out. I call this story, Mr. 'I Got It Right This Time' because this is what a father said to me in court one day. Let me set the stage for that comment. This father, Mr. 'I Got It Right This Time,' — was not paying his child support as he was ordered. At the show cause hearing, he was found to be in criminal contempt and given a 30-day suspended jail sentence and was also ordered to attend classes at Fathers Forever. Mr. 'I Got It Right' came to a few classes, soon skipped a few, and then stopped coming altogether. After a few months, he was back in court for another show cause hearing because he was out of compliance again with his court order, which, this time, included not coming to Fathers Forever. He was sentenced to ten days in jail and reordered to attend classes at Fathers Forever. After he was released from jail, he started coming to class consistently, participated in class discussions, though his input consisted mainly of complaining about the mother of his child.

He completed the requirements for the class and graduated. About six months later, I was in court again, as we, at Fathers Forever, are there two days a week to give our report to the judge and to receive new referrals. Mr. 'I Got It Right' was there. He gave me a strong handshake with a big grin on his face. I asked him why he was back in court. He said as he pointed to his ex-wife, "She is going to ask the judge to forgive the back child support I owed her." This was roughly $10,000. When I asked him what had happened to change her mind, he said: "I got it right. Mr. G, I did everything you told me to do. I called her, and I apologized for the things I said and did over the years. I told her I was going to stop calling her names, sending her nasty texts, and I was going to be a better father to our son. She didn't believe me at first.

I started spending time with my son. I am not paying all my child support because I can't find a steady job because of my criminal record, but I am sending some money in every month." I had to fight back the tears as I thought this is what it's all about, changing their mindset. The district attorney called the case and explained the details to the judge, including what the mother was requesting. The judge asked why she was requesting to forgive the arrearage. These were her words: "Over the past six months, he has been respectful toward me; he is spending a lot of time with our son, almost every day, and he is sending money when he can. I think he is trying." Then she said, "All I ever wanted was for him to spend time with our son and help him with sports; our son is very gifted." She said one more thing that really made me tear up: "I am not exactly sure what they taught him in that Fathers Forever class, but it worked."

She also requested to stop the ongoing child support. The judge didn't agree to that but agreed to forgive the arrearage and set another review date. We all walked out together after all the documents were signed. She shook my hand and said, "I just wanted to thank you personally for your program. It truly worked." I couldn't stop the tears from flowing this time, and I walked swiftly to the bathroom to get some tissue. This story had a happy ending. We changed his perception, which changed his behavior, which changed his outcome.

In his book, The 7 Habits of Highly Effective People, Stephen Covey states: "If you want small change, work on your behavior, if you want quantum-leap changes, work on your paradigms." Covey described a paradigm as the way we see, understand, and interpret the world around us. In other words, a paradigm has to do with our perception: see, do, and get. What we see equals our perceptions; what we do equals our behaviors, and what we get equals our results. Covey goes on to say—and I am paraphrasing here, "If we are going to change our behavior and results, we might first need a 'paradigm shift' to change what we see." This father no doubt loved his son, but his perception of the mother and his role as a father cast a shadow on his love that prevented him from being the good father he was destined to be. A few Fathers Forever classes—12 to be exact—helped him change his perception, which changed his behavior, which changed his result, and his outcome.

REVISION TIME!

Q. 1. Please fill out the blanks with the most appropriate answer from the brackets.

a) Start to recognize that you have a talent and a gift, and you have something that you can _____. (give, take, offer, demand)

b) You've been beaten up, but your _____ is the same. (integrity, value, stance, dream)

c) If you don't have your _____ in order, you can't take the weight of life, you will get corrupt, and you will explode. (decisions, desire, character, traits)

d) One of the highest _____ that you can have as a father and as a man is to take care of your children and be responsible. (honor, platforms, stance, belief)

e) Begin to empower relationships by being ready to _____. (forgive, apologize, demand, give)

Q. 2. Encircle 'True' or 'False' if you think the statements are right or wrong, respectively.

a) Don't let your talent and your ability be absorbed by your character flaws.

        True   False

b) No doubt, both parents loved their children, but sometimes their perception about the other parent cast a shadow on their love and prevented them from being the loving parents they were destined to be.

        True   False

c) There are things that you can do to get back on track and if you're not there already, forgive and not walk in happiness and joy.

        True   False

d) Don't let your character flaws get in the way and stop you from doing what you were created to do.

        True   False

e) If you haven't recognized the flaws in you, you might not be able to recognize them in your children.

        True   False

Q. 3. Describe in a single line what you have learned by

reading this chapter.

_____

Q. 4. Describe in a single line how you will be applying what you have learned in this chapter.

_____

Answer Key

Q. 1. (a) Start to recognize that you have a talent and a gift, and you have something that you can <u>offer</u>.

b) You've been beaten up, but your <u>value</u> is the same.

c) If you don't have your <u>character</u> in order, you can't take the weight of life, you will get corrupt, and you will explode.

d) One of the highest <u>honors</u> that you can have as a father and as a man is to take care of your children and be responsible.

e) Begin to empower relationships by being ready to <u>apologize</u>.

Q. 2. a) True.

b) True.

c) False.

d) True.

e) False.

Q. 3 & 4. If you do not have an answer, reread the chapter and try to take a lesson from it. There is no right or wrong answer for these.

Chapter 11

Destiny Development, Part 2

Contentious co-parenting can hinder destiny development in children

"The only person you are destined to become is the person you decide to be" are the words spoken by Ralph Waldo Emerson, a great American philosopher and essayist who influenced generations. Emerson has explained that destiny can be created if we take the decision into our own hands, which can only be done when we take control of our lives.

Some actions you take are related to fatherhood which connects with destiny; therefore, it is important to be self-sufficient when carrying out your duties as a father. Budgeting is part of your responsibility so as to take good care of your child and point them toward a life filled with success. Budgeting is part of life. The problem is, sometimes, we have more money going out than coming in, and consequently, we fail to have a proper budget.

When it comes down to the child support world, it's important to have a budget because there are some payments that you have to make. The consequence of not paying your electricity bill is that power to your home gets cut off, and you have to stay in the dark. If you don't pay your phone, bill, your service gets interrupted. You can't make a phone call until you pay the bill. Similarly, child support is a bill, to some degree, to have a relationship with your child. If you don't pay this bill, you can lose everything you've got.

What comes to your mind when you hear the word 'child support'? Is it money? Since money is a major part of it, you are right to think so, but child support is a much broader term and involves supporting your child on every level.

If your child needs shoes or similar stuff that's outside of the scope of child support, then you need to support them, as it is your responsibility to buy them anything they might need. Get involved in areas that would require your support, such as putting money away for their education, showing them how to invest or buy stocks or bonds, and how to save or open up a savings account. All of that is child support which is essential for their lives.

Co-parenting is another major factor as both the parents come together and figure out a way to be there for the kids. What do you think is the likelihood of your kids being successful? If parents work together to make sure a child is taken care of, then that child is more likely to be successful. Both parents need to put their differences aside and focus on their children. They need to come together for the common good of their children. When co-parenting fails, children lose hope and are more prone to feeling conflicted, which leaves them distracted from their studies and other goals.

Unsuccessful co-parenting brings a pause to destiny development because now a child has been struggling with something that they shouldn't be struggling with because of their parents' inability to get along. How much are you going to shape your child's destiny and purpose? If you work together to help your child be successful, the odds go up as the sky is the limit of what your kid could be because they get support from both parents. You might be fighting one another, but if you put your differences aside and let your co-parenting take over effectively, it will result in your child being successful.

Another factor that polishes destiny development is dependability. The question is, can people depend on you? As fathers and as men, we are leaders. The question is, who are you leading and what you're leading them to? Can people depend on you when you tell little Jimmy that you're going to pick him up at four o'clock on a Friday afternoon? Are you there at four o'clock? Is he sitting there with his bag ready to go, but his father never shows up?

I've seen grown people sitting at my desk in my office, crying about things that their fathers didn't do for them. These 40 and 50-year-old men are still carrying around the pain of what their fathers didn't do for them as kids. Do you see the devastating effects of not being a good father to your kids? You tell your kids you're going to be at a certain place and meet them, but you don't show up, you don't even bother calling as you're out with your boys or whatever you're doing and having fun; you think, "I'll call them later." But what about the kid who is waiting for you, hoping you'd show up any minute? If you can't be somewhere, you call your kids and tell them that. Don't keep them waiting.

Things happen, your car could break down, or you might have to stay at work longer than expected. What do you do in such situations? Are you dependable? Do you call your kid and say, "Hey, daddy can't come today. Something came up, but I'll make it up to you." When you say you'll make it up to them, do you keep your word? Be there for them and be a person that can help shape them because when they see that their father is not dependable, the child's destiny and their purpose can be thrown off.

Be dependable as your word is your bond. If you tell somebody something, swear by your heart; that's why you count up the cost before you agree on something.

Reliability is another factor that is essential in developing a child's destiny. If a father is reliable and responsible, there is a higher chance of their children being reliable as well and portray that in their day-to-day life.

Here is another story, 'Show and Tell: The Woodpile.' "Fatherhood is on-the-job training; however, both the trainer and the trainee have to be present for effective training."

'Show and Tell' is usually an activity for school-going children in which each child produces an object and tells something about it. Let's look at the name of the game from a different vantage point. Growing up in a small town that is 30 miles south of Raleigh, we had wood heaters that kept our family of nine warm during the winter months. My father would hitch a trailer to our station wagon, my siblings and I would pile into the car, and we would all go to the lumber yard to get wood at least three times during the winter months.

We would take the wood home and unload it in our

backyard. From the backyard, a smaller pile would be taken to the porch, and from the porch, an even smaller pile would be taken inside the house and stored at a safe distance from the heater. When the fire started to go out, one of us would restock the heater with very little effort. The temperature in our home would remain warm and toasty throughout the day. We were learning lessons in planning, teamwork, and discipline, taught and supervised by our father. When I came of age and got my driving license, my father helped me to hitch a trailer to the station wagon and then allowed me to drive my siblings and myself to the lumber yard to get wood.

Of course, he was there supervising; after all, I was in training. Then the day came that he took off the training wheels. On that day, he told me to hitch a trailer to the station wagon and drive my siblings and me to the lumber yard to get wood, with no supervision from my father. It then became my job to supervise the woodpiles from the lumber yard to the heater and to keep the temperature in our home warm and toasty throughout the day. This brings a new meaning to the term 'Show and Tell.'

My father showed me what to do, then he told me to do it under his supervision. I did it very successfully after he showed me many, many times. According to Proverbs 22:6, we are supposed to train up a child "in the way he should go: and when he is old, he will not depart from it." The word "train" means to discipline, to start the child in the right direction in preparing for his or her future responsibilities.

My father pointed us in the right direction and prepared us for our future responsibilities. Those life lessons were much, much bigger than getting wood from the lumber yard. Parenting/fatherhood is on-the-job training; however, both the trainer and the trainee have to be present for effective training. Lessons in planning, teamwork, and discipline can be taught in classrooms and textbooks, but perhaps sometimes "show and tell" is the best teacher. 'Show and Tell' is still dealing with children; we as parents have to show them what to do, and then tell them to go do it.

REVISION TIME!

Q. 1. Please fill out the blanks with the most appropriate answer from the brackets.

a) The only person you are destined to become is the person you _____ to be. (portray, decide, envision, imagine)

b) The actions you take are all related to fatherhood which connects with destiny; therefore, it is important to be self-sufficient when carrying out your _____ as a father. (duties, demands, needs, wishes)

c) Budgeting is a part of your _____ as you take good care of your child and point them toward a life filled with success. (drive, attitude, dream, responsibility)

d) Child support is a much broader term that is more difficult than _____ as you are supporting your child on every level. (cars, money, rent, eviction)

e) Unsuccessful co-parenting brings a pause to destiny development because now a child has been struggling with something that they shouldn't be struggling with because of mom and dad's _____ to get along. (ability, inability, promise, intention)

Q. 2. Encircle 'True' or 'False' if you think the statements are right or wrong, respectively.

a) When it comes down to the child support world, it's important to have a budget because there are some payments that you have to make.

True   False

b) You might be fighting one another, but if you put your differences aside and let your co-parenting take over non-effectively, it will result in your child being successful.

True   False

c) Be dependable as your word is your bond.

True   False

d) If a father is reliable and responsible, there is a lower chance of their children being reliable as well and portray that in their day-to-day life.

True   False

e) Fatherhood is on-the-job training; however, both the trainer and the trainee have to be present for effective training.

True   False

Q. 3. Describe in a single line what you have learned by reading this chapter.

_____

Q. 4. Describe in a single line how you will be applying what you have learned in this chapter.

_____

Answer Key

Q. 1. a) The only person you are destined to become is the person you <u>decide</u> to be.

b) The actions you take are all related to fatherhood which connects with destiny; therefore, it is important to be self-sufficient when carrying out your <u>duties</u> as a father.

c) Budgeting is part of your <u>responsibility</u> as you take good care of your child and point them toward a life filled with success.

d) Child support is a much broader term that is more difficult than <u>money</u> as you are supporting your child on every level.

e) Unsuccessful co-parenting brings a pause to destiny development because now a child has been struggling with something that they shouldn't be struggling with because of mom and dad's <u>inability</u> to get along.

Q. 2. a) True.

b) False.

c) True.

d) False.

e) True.

Q. 3 & 4. If you do not have an answer, reread the chapter and try to take a lesson from it. There is no right or wrong answer for these.

Chapter 12

The Purpose of Fatherhood

Heaven is like a father caring for the wellbeing of his children.

Writing this book gave me immense pleasure because I'm helping my fellow fathers become better fathers. Children are the shine of one's life. We, as parents, can't imagine a life without them. We are often stuck in situations where we have no idea what we can possibly do to raise these children. It is one difficult task. Emotions are high, time is critical, and there are so many questions that are running through a father's head as to what comes next? We are always worried about whether we are doing a good job as fathers or not.

We are often made to believe that it is a mother's responsibility to raise a child and that her upbringing will have the most effect. However, this is the greatest misconception of all time. Because of this misconception, we often end up hurting our child's future as we think that they do not need us around if the mother is around. Or, as a single parent, we believe that we can put our children in nurseries or get a nanny because they need a female figure more than us.

However, all these concepts are seriously flawed. A child needs his father equally, if not more than the mother. We need to do more to ensure our children grow into healthy human beings that they will become tomorrow. Most children around us go through a difficult phase of life due to traumas they see during their childhood caused by their parents and their conflicts. We, as fathers, must know the consequence of our actions. Our marital conflicts should have minimal effect on the child. Or, as single parents, we must ensure that there is no rock left unturned when it comes to good parenting.

Children from fatherless homes are generally unhappy. Daughters growing up need a good role model as a man who can support and stand with them. Similarly, a son needs good support from his father to show him how to take charge in life. Boys need more rough playing, and when they are robbed off of their father, they will be unable to establish some important life skills later on in their lives. A male father figure is important for both the sexes, so the children understand that there is always someone in their life who is ready to protect them in their most difficult times. While mothers are nurturing and patient with their children, a father needs to establish a role of a protector and guardian. A child is constantly learning; hence it is important to be good fathers who can tell their kids about the importance of life and how one should live ideally. What we teach them during their childhood will become embedded in their minds so much that it will work as a code that they will always practice as they grow up into adults. Hence, a father's role becomes very critical.

As a parent, we always should strive to teach our children the valuable skills that they will need to survive in the times that are ahead of them. Let's face it. The world that they will grow up in will not be an easy one at best. There will be so much at stake, and every little thing will come at a price for them. For example, the world that they will grow up in might have very scarce resources; fewer jobs, more competition, complicated relationships, and life, in general, will be harsh overall. Our job as fathers is to make sure that our child has the skill set, emotional wellbeing, and the right attitude about life to combat these obstacles in the future. As we have discussed in the previous chapters, children expect a lot from their fathers.

I took up the journey of being the lone father myself, which gradually made me realize how crucial and impactful parenting is for a child. Cooking for my three children seemed like a daunting task, and I had no idea what I was doing with it. I realized that a simple task like cooking a meal for your child requires so much thought. Every little thing has to be so well thought out because you have to make sure your child gets whatever he or she needs to grow into strong individuals. When we eat ourselves, we do not think as actively as to what we are consuming. However, as a father, we always have to think about what our child eats. But most of the time, due to the lack of exposure and training on the father's side, we are oblivious as to what to do. Hence I wrote this book to tell all the readers how I did it. And let me tell you that none of it was ever easy. We had to take strong measures, and I had to make a lot of sacrifices. Having a child means their needs always come first, and you have to make sure that their needs are met. For some fathers, being a single parent can be a scary task. I know I have been here; however, let me tell you this clearly, it is all worth it, and it all works out in the end. Children also have a way of guiding us through what it is that they want from us. I think, for me, the biggest lesson while I was parenting was that my life got easier when I communicated with my children well enough. Sometimes we do not know what is going on and what they are going through, and due to the age difference, it is harder for us to understand, but if we have clear communication channels with them, we will surely know how to be the perfect father for them. Trust your gut; it is often right when it comes to your kids.

One of the purposes of a father is to show and teach his children how to handle life, the good, bad, and the ugly. Consider this story.

In my days as a single father, I had to learn how to cook, and I did, Since cooking was a new thing to me, I hadn't invested in any cookware, so I just used what I had, which was mainly "hand me down" pots and pans.

In one of the pots given to me, the handle was loose, and every time I used it, it would get loser and loser. I kept meaning to get a screwdriver and tighten it, but I kept procrastinating and never did.

Then one day, I boiled some eggs to make an egg salad; as I attempted to move the hot pot from the stove to the sink, the handle came off, the pot full of very hot boiling water, and six boiled eggs came crashing down to the floor and my feet. I managed to minimize the burn to my feet by jumping back; however, I didn't escape all of the hot water.

As I sat nursing my burnt feet, two thoughts came to me; one was how important pot handles are and how my

214

negligence toward getting it fixed on time caused me second-degree burns and pain to my feet, and how it could've been a lot worse than that.

I want to make a correlation between fathers and pot handles, as you may have already guessed. The first point is, pot handles are very important and necessary. They allow you to move a very hot pot, full of boiling water from one place to the other, safely, whenever and wherever you want, without getting burned. Fathers, we are essential and necessary as well; we have to show and teach our children how to handle life's "hot pots" safely as they transition from one place to another in life.

The second point, the pot was very hot, and the water in the pot was boiling, but the handle wasn't hot at all; however, due to my procrastination, I caused the handle to be separated from the pot, which caused me pain. Fathers, don't let negligence separate you from protecting your children. Sometimes life gets very hot, and it's the father's responsibility to become the handle that safeguards his children from the "hot pots" of life so they don't get burned.

Without that pot handle, it would've been very difficult and dangerous for me to move that "hot pot" from one point to another. As fathers, we are to teach our children on a regular basis how to handle life "hot pots" because if we are not there to teach them, how will they learn? How will they know? Life's "hot pots" could be very difficult and dangerous for them as well. Perhaps that's why many of our children are getting first, second, and third-degree life burns because out of our negligence. Because we are not there.

The point is, we are supposed to teach our children and families how to handle life. If we don't, it could have devastating effects on them and cause pain, just as my negligence caused pain to my feet. So the next time you see a pot handle, FATHERS, remember these three things; first, you are to teach your children how to handle life's "hot pots," second, sometimes you have to become the handles that keep them from getting burned by the "hot pots," and third, the pot and the handle have to stay connected at all times. I want you to keep this analogy in your mind at all times when you are raising your children.

The purpose of fatherhood has been changing over time. For many years, fathers thought that their primary role was to provide for the family, enforce authority, and get obedience in return from the children. However, these are ancient practices and modern parenting objects to this kind of way of raising children. Why should your child be obedient to you at the expense of their personal freedom? Such parenting restricts the child from growing into their full potential, and now science realizes that these strict boundaries may negatively impact your child, which you need to avoid. As dads in today's world, we understand we need to be better than our fathers. We need to adapt to a different parenting strategy. Yes, we still need to provide for our children as their primary care falls on us; however, it should not be at the expense of their personal freedom. The element of nurturing and providing has to run side by side in order for us to do well as fathers. Gone are the days where children were fearful of us in terms of strict obedience. Instead, fatherhood should be all about sharing experiences of life with our children and vice versa. Though we are their protectors and teach them discipline, discipline does not have to come with force and fear. Today fatherhood is all about taking those baby steps with our children and helping them grow into adults with sound judgment, good mental health, and a positive outlook in life. Fatherhood is about giving love to our children just as a mother gives to the child. There is no masculinity in being less loving toward our offspring; it is an important way of life. Today, fatherhood is also about self-betterment; we can no longer be slack and do less than we have the potential for. This is because we have a child who looks up to us. We have to be

217

excellent examples in order to be role models for our children. If we have bad habits like excessive drinking, those will impact our children too. Hence when we reach fatherhood, we no longer have room to entertain bad habits because that will only negatively impact our children, and we don't want that, do we?

REVISION TIME!

Q. 1. Please fill out the blanks with the most appropriate answer from the brackets.

a) It is never an easy ___ to raise children. (praise, job, day)

b) You need to let go of all your _____ to raise your children. (life, time, bad habits)

c) Raising children requires a lot of _____. (courage, patience, power)

d) When you cook a meal for your child, make sure it meets their ____. (food, nutritional needs, time)

e) A child _____ needs their father if not more than a mother. (half, equally, wholesome)

Q.2. What did you learn in this chapter? Briefly explain.

_____

Q.3. How will you use this book to better your parenting style?

_____

Answer Key

Q. 1. a) It is never an easy <u>job</u> to raise children.

b) You need to let go of all your <u>bad habits</u> to raise your children.

c) Raising children requires a lot of <u>patience</u>.

d) When you cook a meal for your child, make sure it meets their <u>nutritional needs.</u>

e) A child <u>equally</u> needs their father if not more than a mother.

Q. 2 & 3. If you do not have an answer, reread the chapter and try to take a lesson from it. There is no right or wrong answer for these.